Praise for

MW00574317

The American people need to understand that we are operating under an administrative state form of government cloaked with an illusion of a republic. To understand how we got here, and how we return to a constitutional republic, you need to read *American Leviathan*.

—JESSE KELLY, host of *The Jesse Kelly Show*

Ned Ryun's *American Leviathan* identifies the threat—the metastasizing administrative state that is killing America and the American Dream. Insightful and inspiring, American Leviathan sets out the terms of battle and lays out a plan to recover our country from the faceless, mindless pinko bureaucrats who have presumed to take it over. Every American citizen needs to read Ned Ryun's *American Leviathan*.

—KURT SCHLICHTER, senior columnist for Townhall.com

While the left has spent years screaming about protecting "democracy," their real goal is dismantling the constitution so that we are governed by unelected and unaccountable bureaucrats in the federal government. Ned Ryun's compelling and terrifying *American Leviathan* pulls the curtain back and exposes all the ways authoritarian radicals in the administrative state are impossible to fire and divorced from political accountability, but still wield awesome power to write rules and regulations that are ruining your life and livelihood. Ultimately, the greatest threat to our freedoms and way of life isn't China, isn't Russia. It's America's bureaucratic Leviathan crushing the life out of the American people.

—MOLLIE HEMINGWAY, editor-in-chief for The Federalist

Whether you call it 'The Deep State' or 'The Permanent Political Class' or 'The Out-Of-Control Bureaucracy', it's become very clear that 'THEY' control our government, 'THEY' act as an internal resistance to any reform-minded, duly-elected official and 'THEY' will do whatever it takes to keep the power 'THEY' have amassed. In *American Leviathan* Ned Ryun brilliantly exposes who they are, where they came from, how they amassed treated power and subversive plans under Barack Obama, and, most importantly, how to remove them from their unconstitutional positions of power. *American Leviathan* is a must-read for any politician in Washington DC who takes seriously their oath to 'protect and defend the constitution from all enemies foreign and domestic.'

—LARRY O'CONNOR, nationally known radio host at WMAL and Townhall Media

American Leviathan makes it powerfully clear that it's time for the American people to decide whether we will be obedient serfs in the feudal administrative state, or whether we will choose to reclaim our rights as freeborn Americans and live in a self-governing republic. Ned Ryun charts the course with this fantastic book.

—PETE HEGSETH, co-host of *FOX & Friends Weekend* and author of *The War on Warriors*

The cancerous Administrative State is eating us alive. Unaccountable bureaucrats, insulated from the impact of their own tyranny, are destroying our Republic. *American Leviathan* details the rise of the Administrative State and how it can be deconstructed. But that deconstruction will only happen if we understand what is happening and demand a return to a Constitutional Republic.

—DAN BONGINO, host of the *Dan Bongino Show*

There are two competing governments in America today: the remnants of the original Constitutional Republic and a permanent, unaccountable Administrative State. Donald J. Trump revealed the existence of the latter and made it clear that the two systems cannot co-exist. One system must do away with the other. The question is this: Will the American people finally surrender to the anti-American permanent bureaucracy or reclaim their rights in full as free-born people?

—SEBASTIAN GORKA PhD, host of *AMERICA First* and former strategist to President Trump

AMERICAN
LEVIATHAN

THE BIRTH OF THE ADMINISTRATIVE STATE
AND PROGERESSIVE AUTHORITARIANISM

NED RYUN

BOOKS

New York • London

First American edition published in 2024 by Encounter Books,
an activity of Encounter for Culture and Education, Inc.,
a nonprofit, tax-exempt corporation.
www.encounterbooks.com
Manufactured in the United States and printed on
acid-free paper. The paper used in this publication meets
the minimum requirements of Ansi/niso Z39.48–1992 (r 1997)
(*Permanence of Paper*).

FIRST AMERICAN EDITION

LIBRARY OF CONGRESS CATALOGING-IN-PUBLICATION
DATA ISAVAILABLE

Information for this title can be found
at the Library of Congress website under the following

ISBN 9781641774376 AND LCCN 2024942274.

To Becca, my wife and my best friend.

Leviathan (n) le· vi· a· than

1a:A sea monster defeated by Yahweh in various Scriptural accounts.

2: The political state, especially a totalitarian state, having a vast bureaucracy.

CONTENTS

AUTHOR'S NOTE

America's Progressive Statists have always been of great interest to me, not only because of their tremendous ability to organize at the state and local level, which is something we do at American Majority, but also because of how they systematically and very intentionally changed our government and society fundamentally over a century ago. It is apparent, from even a cursory reading of their writings and superficial understanding of their philosophy of government, and then from the birth of their bureaucratic administrative state, that they have very little, if anything, in common with the Founders of the free American Republic and the original intent of their Constitution and Bill of Rights.

At American Majority, we've taught on some of this in the past with our "The System" presentation, but my entire experience in dealing with the fallout of the Trump/Russia collusion hoax on MSNBC, CNN, and other outlets began to raise even more questions as to what was really taking place in America. Taking a step back, looking at its entirety, and considering my several decades in Washington, DC, I started asking questions about many things: how did we get here as a country, and what is this really about? Because so-called Russian collusion was the last thing all of that breathless pearl clutching was about. That was simply the pretext for something else, something much larger at play. This questioning, of course, eventually led to this book.

I have several goals in writing *American Leviathan*. The first is that people understand in as concise a way as possible the story of how we got to where we are as a country in the 21st century. It's a story that begins well over a hundred years ago, but one that needs to be understood for people to fully grasp where we are in America today. My hope is that there will be a shift in how people view their current government and that they will in essence put on another "pair of glasses" through which they view the world and, awakening from their slumber, realize that what we are experiencing in this country today has very little to do with the American Republic as originally intended.

Another goal was of course to move the Overton Window on the un-American Left, who tend to use the term "Progressive" as a positive. It shouldn't be seen as a positive, *ergo* my intentional and consistent use of the appellation Progressive *Statists*. Every Progressive is an adherent to and believer in the "progress" towards a powerful and eventually invasive and authoritarian state that will enforce equity and social justice and, they naively believe, achieve the perfection of humanity. It must be understood, as the noted Progressive Herbert Croly stated, that the Progressive ideas of democracy rise and fall on the perfectibility of man, on human nature's being elevated to a higher plane. Progressive Statists justify their massive state apparatus by this belief and then attempt to do a *kabuki* dance and color over the invasive authoritarianism that such a massive state entails with various and vapid platitudes about democracy and bettering all human beings. However, there is no denying they adhere to the all-powerful state as the ultimate solution—and are either unwilling to admit it, or are being completely disingenuous in admitting the truth in hopes they in fact will be the Ruling Class as everyone else is forced to bow the knee to them and to the state.

I would hope that readers of this book will absolutely see the world differently and that they too will question everything. The only way we return to a true republic is for enough of the American people to question the premise and legitimacy of the administrative state, because that will be the beginning of the end for it.

This questioning, of course, is intended to lead not to anarchy but to a pursuit of truth and then, more importantly, action spurred on and compelled by that truth. We must ask ourselves in the 21st century: what is the right government for the American people? We must accept that there is a need for government; we're no angels, and we in our imperfect nature cannot be left to our own devices.

But what is the right size and scope of government for us today? That's the real question and one that needs to be fleshed out, starting from the notions that government should be limited in size and scope; that those unelected bureaucrats who staff the government are actually beneath and accountable to the peoples' duly elected representatives; that those representatives delegated authority by the American people are the ones who should actually be governing; and that the government which is of, by, and for the people should actually work to advance the interests and priorities of the American people.

These are all deeply fundamental questions for which there are potential solutions. But change begins with rejecting the premise that the status quo is right or legitimate. Once that starting point is agreed upon, then the courage to pursue the right solutions should follow. My hope is that more and more people will reject the legitimacy of the administrative state in this country, which is truly the American Leviathan; accept once again the primacy of the constitutional Republic with its limited size and scope and its diffusion and separation of powers; and return to a firm belief in and commitment to the idea that the American people should be first and last in all things.

Keep America Free,
Ned Ryun
Elysium Farm, 2024

CHAPTER ONE

IN MEDIAS RES

You must question everything because it is only in questioning that you can discover the truth. And there are many questions that must be asked about the current state of America.

How did we get to where we are as a country today? How is it that the duly elected president of the United States can be targeted by the Department of Justice and the FBI based off a fabricated, fake dossier that those doing the targeting, knowing it was fake, still used to secure four FISA warrants in a massive abuse of power—and yet no one suffered consequences for it? How can former President Trump have his home at Mar-a-Lago thuggishly raided on the thinnest of pretenses while another president, Joe Biden, gets a free pass on his handling of classified documents? How do concerned parents showing up at school board meetings to question the curriculum being used to indoctrinate their children end up being considered domestic terrorists by powerful elements of their government?

How is it that dozens and dozens of pro-life centers are firebombed and no one is arrested, yet dozens of peaceful pro-life protesters get early morning raids from heavily armed FBI agents? How do we end up with incompetents such as Dr. Anthony Fauci, who knew and knows nothing, declaring "I am the science" and being treated like an oracle of God?

But even more so, how did we get a government so far removed from the people, in a country supposedly governed of, by, and for the people? Only the naive still believe that our government prioritizes the best interests of the American people or, for that matter, even really considers them. It's also worth asking if most Americans really understand that their duly elected president doesn't really run and control the US government. And since that is the reality, ask yourself when was the last time you met a real decision-maker in DC: not an elected official, but a real decision-maker in one of the vast and powerful departments and agencies.

The answer is probably never.

Why is all of this so, and how did we end up here? None of it would make sense if we were actually living in a constitutional republic. So we must first accept that we are living something of a lie, an illusion, in the United States. The lie began over a century ago that somehow this country is still a constitutional republic as intended by our Founders that summer of 1787. The lie has been hiding, lurking underneath the surface for decades, as two opposing governing views, complete polar opposites of each other, have pulled, pushed, and collided for much of the 20th century and now into the 21st.

The friction between these two competing views has been bubbling up over time. Those paying attention question how what takes place in DC on a daily basis has anything to do with how the free American Republic is supposed to operate. The truth of this and the tension between the two governing views suddenly burst into the open in 2017.

That spring, Washington, DC, was consumed with talk of Russian collusion on the part of President Donald J. Trump. Supposedly, the story went (or more precisely, the fairytale), Russian President Vladimir Putin had influenced the 2016 election in Trump's favor through social-media ad buys, albeit infinitesimally small, and other channels of influence and leverage over Trump to make sure he got his puppet into the White House. There was breathless, ad nauseam talk of compromising incidents in Moscow with the then-businessman Trump, supposed *kompromat* as detailed in the infamous Steele Dossier. But the narrative, when boiled down to its essence, was that Trump had been inserted into the most powerful office on earth by an enemy of the country and, thanks to the potential for blackmail, was nothing less than Putin's puppet. It's so absurd on its face that only in a country where most of the corporate media appears to be stenographers for the intelligence community would such a thing ever be pushed as legitimate.

Looking back on it now, you might find it hard to believe how any serious, sane person accepted the story as true. But the DC "news media" would breathlessly report new, "breaking" details almost every day from unnamed, anonymous sources (think intel community), with TV chyrons flashing some variation of "Trump Russia Collusion" day after day, week after week, and then month after mind-numbing month. From the nightly screeds on MSNBC explaining that somehow Trump was a traitor to his country, to Pulitzers awarded to the *New York Times* and *Washington Post* for their "groundbreaking" reporting on the issue, the entire Acela corridor from DC to New York was consumed with the story, convinced it was real or at least giving the impression they thought it was real. But even more so, they were determined to make the American people believe it was real.

But then the collusion conspiracy theory began to unravel.

When Attorney General Jeff Sessions was preposterously targeted and questioned about his own Russian connections and interactions, he obediently recused himself, as all controlled and weak GOP types do. Robert Mueller, the former head of the FBI, was appointed as special counsel by Deputy Attorney General Rod Rosenstein to investigate Trump and Russia collusion. However, despite his team of wolfish and rabid partisans, led by Andrew Weissmann and empowered with every government resource and $40 million in funding, over the course of nearly eighteen months, Mueller found absolutely no evidence of collusion on any level.

Under further scrutiny it became abundantly clear that the much-vaunted and -invoked Steele Dossier was nothing more than cut-and-pasted conspiracy theories, with "evidence" fed to the gullible former British spy Christopher Steele by Igor Danchenko, who was "later indicted for lying to the FBI and whom a special counsel investigation showed was tied to Russian intelligence."[1] Steele, however, was apparently more than happy to be a conduit for Russian misinformation that was then happily amplified by our FBI and Intel Community. Even worse, it became clear that Steele and his dossier, working hand in hand with the manufactured news entity of Fusion GPS, had been in fact one of the dirtiest tricks in American politics, funded by the DNC and the Hillary Clinton campaign to help try and take Trump down, with the DOJ and FBI more than happy to oblige and work towards the same goal.

The appalling nature of the entire situation was apparently lost on many Americans, thanks in no small part to the corporate propagandists and state stenographers obfuscating the facts. Knowing early on that the Steele Dossier was likely bogus did not prevent the heavily politicized FBI, led by the sanctimonious James Comey, from using the dossier not once or twice but four times in securing FISA warrants to spy on the minor Trump campaign advisor Carter Page, a backdoor for expanding its "intelligence" operations on President-Elect and then President Trump. Again, all of this was done to bring down the duly elected president of the United States.

It was nothing less than a slow-moving coup against the president of the United States. In the opinion of the administrative state's ruling class and its allies in the Democratic Party and the corporate-propaganda apparatus, the wrong person had won the 2016 presidential election.

And yet, despite everything, after years of feeding frenzies, Pulitzers, investigations, and the world-is-ending mentality of many on TV and the Left, once Mueller testified in front of Congress that there was no proof of any Russian collusion, exonerating Trump, the allegations and stories and frenzy just floated and faded away. Today many of those same people who spent years accusing the president of the United States of being a traitor to his country, who bought wholesale laughable conspiracy theories, act as though it never happened. But even more so, God forbid, they would never even think of apologizing for being completely, utterly wrong about it all. Why? What was that all about? What was this phenomenon that consumed DC and New York City ultimately about?

It had nothing to do with facts or reality. When everything else is peeled away, the Russian Collusion fairytale had nothing to actually do with Russia, collusion, or anything else except one fundamental issue: *who decides.*

When Donald Trump pulled off a stunning upset in the 2016 presidential election, he arrived in DC under the impression that as the duly elected president of the United States he would be the one directing foreign and domestic policy for his administration, and by that the direction of the government and the country writ large. He of course was correct in thinking that in a constitutional republic, as the American Founders intended for this country, that is precisely how things are supposed to work.

In theory, our Republic is supposed to operate thus: all power flows from the people to their elected representatives, who are made the stewards of the money and power given to them by the people to enact a government and policies that advance and promote the interests of the American people. In fact, it is the moral imperative of a nation's leaders to prioritize the national interests of the people. To do otherwise is immoral. In the Republic, there is some level of accountability because those elected representatives have to face the people at the polling booth at regularly scheduled times: every two years for the House, four for the president, and six for the Senate. In theory, if said elected representatives are not carrying out the will of the people, i.e., being immoral, then they can be replaced by the election process, although over the years they have in fact insulated themselves as much as they can from accountability. This is how it is supposed to work. It was under this impression that the Great Outsider, Trump, showed up in DC.

And that understanding of how things are supposed to work in Washington, DC, is exactly what Trump got completely wrong.

Of course, he should be forgiven for his "mistake" because, technically, we are still living under the US Constitution and the constitutional republic that flows from it. Only that's not how it works anymore in DC. Some would say that in reality, the constitutional republic is a quaint relic of an era gone by, more of an illusion than anything else. We might still throw about such phrases as "separation of powers," "three branches of government," "government of, by, and for the people," and all the other familiar terms we read, or should we say once read, in civics and history books, but the reality is far, far different from all of that.

How Washington, DC, and our government work in fact entails a diametrically opposite approach to governing than a republic. In reality we are governed by an administrative-state approach in which an unelected, detached, powerful bureaucracy, filled with a supposedly educated elite, are the ones who decide, who actually govern. It was a rude awakening for Trump when he confronted this reality. Instead of running the US government, he found himself at incessant war with certain powerful elements of it who fought him every day—in fact, doing their best to see him removed from office since they viewed him as an existential threat to the entire edifice of the administrative state, all because he rejected the premise of it.

How did we get here?

Not by chance, but very intentionally. As envisioned and planned by the Progressive Statists over a century ago, these unelected bureaucrats were to do the true governing in America. What we have in reality today is exactly what was supposed to happen according to the Progressive

Statists' fevered dreams of utopia and the perfection of man on earth, which have led to the birth of the administrative state. The unelected "educated elite" were in fact always meant to be the "deciders" in government. They were, and are, to be separated from accountability to We the People, insulated from the "dirty corrupting influence" of politics, and allowed to run the government as they see fit from their perch of supposedly disinterested and educated elitism, since they know what's best for this country.

Embraced by both major parties at the turn of the 20th century (truly the beginning of the Uniparty in DC), the new Progressive Statist philosophy of governing, which was nothing less than a regime change against and over the Constitution of 1787, clearly rejected the Founders' Republic. With the acceptance of their ideas by the American populace in the 1912 presidential election, the Progressive Statists set in motion a transformation of American government and society as a whole.

Because of how the power and decision-making was intended to work inside the Progressives' administrative state, over the course of the last century, elected representatives, the supposed stewards of the people's power and money, have become more stewards of the state than the representatives of the people. As they obediently fund the state with increasing amounts of taxpayer dollars, they act more as the middle men between the people and the state, providing little oversight or accountability to a massive and sprawling entity. It's become apparent over the course of the 20th century and into the 21st that the real form and function of governing has been transferred over to the unelected administrative-state managerial class.

In many ways, over the last century our elected officials have gone from being the representatives of the people to stewards and managers of the administrative state, and then, one could argue, to almost serving the state themselves. The sound and fury of politics and regular elections only serve to mark time, providing an illusion of form while the real substance and business is done by the state and its increasingly powerful and unaccountable unelected bureaucrats whose priorities many times have nothing to do with the American people's.

Once this reality has dawned and one sees the world through the correct lenses, it really comes into focus as bizarre *kabuki* theatre. Many politicians loudly proclaim that they will go to DC and bring accountability or devolve power but end up funding the state and its governing class who are consolidating more power, who are in fact making more policy. The supposed stewards of the peoples' money and power are actually ceding more control to the state on nearly every front.

It appears the only real difference between the two major political parties in America today is how quickly each thinks the administrative state and its managerial class will grow and how quickly it should obtain complete control of Washington, DC, if it hasn't already. This is the case because, for the most part, both parties and the majority of their elected representatives have accepted the premise that the administrative-state governing philosophy is somehow legitimate. In short, they have accepted the rules of the game being played for the last century in DC—and it is clear to anyone that those who make the rules control the game. It's worth stating the obvious since apparently many in Republican circles haven't yet had this epiphany: you cannot win a game if the opposition has rigged the rules to favor them.

So what in fact took place in 2017, when everything else is peeled away, was the tension between two very different governing approaches— a constitutional republic versus an administrative state—exploding to the surface after a hundred years, all triggered an old-school outsider. Donald Trump, acting under the premise of the Constitution unlike many of his Republican predecessors inside the White House, turned everything on its head in DC with his "shocking" talk of America First and the apparently novel idea that somehow a government *of, by,* and *for* the people, *funded* by the people, should actually work to *benefit* the people on all things: trade, immigration, spending, foreign policy, in fact, everything. In short, Trump was proposing the constitutional, populist, common-sense idea that the American people, especially the American taxpayer, should be first and last in all things.

For rejecting the premise of the administrative state, for having the temerity to essentially announce, "I decide," for challenging powerful bureaucrats, Donald J. Trump was targeted as a traitor to his country—not because he was a traitor on any level, but because he was in fact a patriot. It was that he dared to operate under the constitutional republican philosophy and not that of the administrative state (bolstered by its Progressive Democrat allies and, quite frankly, many inside the establishment Republican Party).

And despite Trump leaving the White House after the highly questionable 2020 elections, the fight continues because Trump refuses to accept the premise that the administrative state decides. Because he is an existential threat to the future of the administrative state should he win re-election to the presidency, it continues to attack him, as seen, for instance, with the weaponized DOJ and FBI targeting him with a raid at Mar-a-Lago.

We got to this point as a country gradually, by degrees, and then suddenly. Some would argue that many in DC were done with representative democracy a century ago, despite many of the first Progressive Statists loudly proclaiming their love of democracy while pushing for a detached and unelected bureaucratic state that was and is deeply undemocratic. For the Progressive Statists the democratic process was inefficient and messy, and the dirty little peasants didn't know what was best for them anyway. Better by far to have the educated elite actually doing the business of governing via the practice of applied science with governmental power consolidated into the administrative state. All of this, mind you, would unfold with as little oversight from politicians as possible because the accountability of elected politics would corrupt the pure process of the noble and unbiased elites, who would be fully focused on doing what was best for the country, in order to solve all human and governmental conflicts and achieve utopia here on earth.

So now suddenly we Americans find ourselves fully exposed to the perhaps startling reality that we are experiencing the illusion of a republic when we are in fact living the Progressive dream of an administrative state. One might argue that the arrangement is all the more insidious because the form and function on the surface look somewhat the same as a republic did, when in fact the whole government has been hollowed out by Progressive Statist termites. The essence is something dramatically different.

Even more so, as the free American Republic has changed so dramatically over the last century, it isn't overly dramatic to state that the Progressive administrative state and its governing philosophy is a gradual, creeping revolution against the Republic and the American people in which the vestiges of the Republic were never truly torn down in a violent, frontal assault coup, but quietly, by degrees, changed in essence—all of course to achieve a revolution, where the old order is thrown down and a new order raised. So we must ask ourselves: what if we were to view the Progressive administrative state as being in complete defiance of the Founders' Republic, which was clearly stated by its originators at the turn of the 20th century, and as nothing less than slow-moving regime change against the Republic, gradually and quietly without real debate?

Because that is precisely what it is.

That is the *thing*, the core issue of what is at stake today in this country. But for us to understand how we got here, how we got this massive, choking beast, the American Leviathan, that daily crushes the freedom and rights of the American people, we must begin at the beginning, at the turn of the 20th century and the rise of the Progressive Statist movement. For we must understand what happened before we can fully reject the entire premise of the unconstitutional administrative state.

CHAPTER TWO

———

WE MUST BEGIN
AT THE BEGINNING

To really understand how we ended up were we are today, from slow-moving coups against the duly elected president of the United States to Dr. Anthony Fauci's declaring he is "the science" as the so-called experts floundered from one debacle to the next in addressing COVID-19, to bureaucrats' meddling with gas stoves or combustion engines or fossil fuels, thinking they are justified in invading every aspect our lives, we have to go back to the late 19th century and the rise of what was the beginning of a Uniparty governing philosophy: the Progressive Statist movement in the United States.

Progressive Statism was really a movement birthed out of the disillusionment of the post–Civil War era in which American intellectuals began to doubt and undermine the entire constitutional republic, questioning whether it had the answers for a rapidly changing world and economy. The movement came out of this economic and societal upheaval and developed into a broad-based social reform movement. Over time, while some of their ideas and actions addressed real societal injustices (for example, corrupt railroad corporations and poor food quality), Progressive Statists, rooted in a worldview far removed from that of the American Founders, completely rejected the constitutional republic, believing it arrived at the wrong remedy for the challenges that faced America in a modern world.

It was a movement that in many ways was birthed inside the Republican Party by the likes of Wisconsin's Robert La Follette, who decried the "unholy alliance" between business and government, and Theodore Roosevelt, who became the leading "evangelist" for the Progressive Statist movement. The Progressive Statists agreed with most Americans that everyone—the worker as well as the business owner—should have a fair opportunity to succeed. The Progressives, however, argued that a truly democratic government should not just protect equal opportunities, but should also be empowered to step in and regulate business practices and social conditions as necessary in order to *guarantee* equal opportunity and, quite frankly, with their ideas regarding private property and redistribution, equal outcomes to all. For that to be accomplished, a massive administrative state had to be formed and funded to achieve what they termed "social justice" (which is not a new term).

As there really was no ability to attain advanced degrees in the limited university or college system in the United States during the late 19th century, most Progressive intellectuals chose to go overseas and study in European universities, especially in Germany for their PhDs. There they were immersed in Georg Hegel's governing philosophy of historicism and Prussian Statism and began to believe that Hegel and his ideas were in fact the solution to America's problems. In Hegel's approach (to be discussed in more detail later), power was fully vested in the state and its departments, which were filled with a powerful managerial class doing the real governing, to advance the priorities of the state and its ruling class. For Hegel, the all-powerful state, filled with an educated elite expertly guiding a nation, was the "march of God on earth." This "enlightened state" was the entire end of the constant, upward, linear march of history, culminating in the perfection of mankind.

It is this Hegelian philosophy that was injected into the American way of life in the late 19th and early 20th century as these Progressive Statists returned to America and began to systematically argue for a complete change in American government. The movement began to ascend in the late 1800s at the state and local level, led by men (and women) of both political parties, but four in particular stand out for their influence in making Progressive Statism a dominant governing philosophy in America.

THE FOUR HORSEMEN OF THE PROGRESSIVE APOCALYPSE

While Progressive Statism had many proponents from both major parties and advocates from all aspects of life, there was a small handful of men who, because of power, position, and influence, should be considered the Four Horsemen of the Progressive Apocalypse: Woodrow Wilson, Robert La Follette, Herbert Croly, and Theodore Roosevelt. These men, who heavily influenced American politics at the turn of the 20th century, were at the forefront of the direct assault on the Founders' Constitution. And in many ways, they were extremely successful in achieving their Progressive Statist goals.

Woodrow Wilson's Study of Administration

One of the leading intellectuals for the Progressive movement, Woodrow Wilson, is today primarily known as a two-term president, but he actually began his career inside of academia, first at Bryn Mywr in Pennsylvania and later as the president of Princeton, from which he then launched his bid for governor of New Jersey. After one term as governor, Wilson made a successful campaign for the White House, winning in 1912. While Wilson was lauded in his day, recent exploration of his bigotry and racism, as well as his authoritarian tendencies, have diminished his legacy greatly.

It was Wilson's writings and speeches in the 1880s and 1890s, in tandem with others, that really began fleshing out the political philosophy and governing approach of the Progressive Statists in America. In 1887, Wilson published his *Study of Administration*, which lays out the idea of a massive bureaucracy of agencies, detached from the political process and "corrupting" influence of politics, that would allow the educated bureaucrats, using their applied science, to bring about actual progress in America.

In his *Study*, heavily influenced by Hegel's ideas, Wilson freely admits that the philosophy of agencies, bureaucracies filled with educated elites and a managerial class, is "a foreign science.... It has been developed by French and German professors, and inconsequently in all parts adapted to the needs of a compact state and made to fit highly *centralized* forms of government" (emphasis added).[1] Wilson lauds the examples of Prussia, "Where administration has been most studied and most nearly perfected," and France under Napoleon, which to Wilson was an "example of the perfecting of civil machinery by the single will of an absolute ruler before the dawn of a constitutional era. No corporate, popular will could have effected arrangements such as those which Napoleon commanded."[2]

Later in his work, Wilson asks what was it that has prevented an administrative state in America? He admits "popular sovereignty," since its "harder for democracy to organize administration than for monarchy." As is the case in all forms of statism, the statists eventually grow frustrated, then tired of, and then antagonistic towards, the representative democratic process in which the people have a real voice and real influence.

After arguing for consolidation of power into administrators, Wilson then contends that the supposed nonpartisan bureaucrats must be protected from the sphere of politics: "Most important to be observed is the truth already so much and so fortunately insisted upon by our civil-service reformers; namely that administration lies *outside* the proper sphere of politics" (emphasis added). Wilson goes on to say that these managers, given great power, detached from politics and oversight from elected representatives, should nevertheless be trusted, as "there is no danger in power, if only it be not irresponsible." In fact, "The greater his power the less likely he is to abuse it, the more is he nerved and sobered and elevated by it." That line encapsulates much of the flawed thinking of Progressives writ large, that somehow imperfect human beings entrusted with significant power would never abuse it.

This idea of a powerful class of bureaucrats removed from political oversight to provide guidance to governance and to really society writ large was central to Wilson's thinking: "Bureaucracy can exist only where the *whole service of the state is removed from the common political life of the people, its chiefs as well as its rank and file. Its motives, its objects, its policy, its standards, must be bureaucratic*" (emphasis added).[3] Put another way, for Wilson's vision to work, administrative bureaucracy must be separated and insulated from politics and the accountability of political elections.

Wilson's arguments helped provide some of the intellectual foundation, but also the practical application, of what Progressive Statism would look like. In short, the creation of a massive administrative state managed by an educated, elite, managerial class, granted the power to use applied science to the world around them and freed from political oversight and the corrupting influence of politics to bring about progress, is the essence of Progressive Statism.

It was at its heart a complete rejection of the Founders' ideas of government. Even more importantly, it was a rejection of the Founders' view of human nature. In trusting individuals with great power and in arrogantly and naively believing those being entrusted with that power would somehow always be driven by noble aspirations, that somehow individuals with that power would never ever think of abusing it, Wilson was not alone.

He was joined by many leading intellectuals on both sides of the political aisle in advancing Progressivism. As Wilson was airing his ideas, Robert La Follette in Wisconsin was intent on actually turning them into reality by winning the governorship and implementing his Progressive Wisconsin Plan, based in many ways on Hegel's Prussian Statism.

CHAPTER THREE

ROBERT LA FOLLETTE
AND HIS WISCONSIN PLAN

A s Wilson, a lifelong Democrat, agitated for Progressive "reform" on the East Coast, the movement was also rising in the Midwest as well. On July 4, 1897, "Fighting" Bob La Follette, a lifelong Republican, climbed up into the back of a buckboard wagon to overlook the crowd gathered for the July 4th celebration in Mineral Point, Wisconsin. A former two-term district attorney for Dane County and three-term Republican congressman, La Follette was in the midst of his third campaign for governor of Wisconsin.

In the early 1890s, he'd become disillusioned with the Republican Party in Wisconsin. He was convinced that it had lost its moral compass, abandoning its principles to become nothing but a surrogate and tool for the railroads and other corporate interests. So in 1894 La Follette, determined to challenge the status quo, defied the will of the party bosses and ran for the Republican gubernatorial nomination. He lost. He ran again in 1896. And lost again. But instead of considering his reform a lost cause, La Follette and his allies, dubbed "The Insurgents," were determined to break the party machine, "The Stalwarts," and their hold over the nomination process of the Republican Party.

Central to La Follette's gubernatorial platform was the idea that real reform was needed in the political process, centered on the undue influence of the corporations on the political machines. He began his speech that day in Mineral Springs by stating:

> The basic principle of this government is the will of the people. A system was devised by its founders which seemed to insure the means of ascertaining that will and of enacting it into legislation and supporting it through the administration of the law. This was to be accomplished by electing men to make, and men to execute, the laws, who, would represent in the laws so made and executed the will of the people.[1]

La Follette had been a Republican since he could remember, and remained as such, but his experience with the Republican Party machine in Wisconsin had given him pause. He'd seen firsthand the party machine dictate who the candidates would be, with the political bosses in reality forcing their will on the voters. What had become apparent to La Follette was that the political bosses were virtually inseparable from the corporations; in his thinking, the party bosses were really nothing more than subsidiaries of the corporations, who with money and favors induced the bosses to nominate candidates favorable to the themselves.

In La Follette's view, the entire game was rigged for the benefit of the corporations:

> Since the birth of the Republic, indeed almost within the last generation, a new and powerful factor has taken its place in our business, financial and political world and is there exercising a tremendous influence. The existence of the corporation, as we have it with us today, was never dreamed of by the fathers.... These corporations, not content with taking royal tribute daily

from the private citizen, shift upon him the chief support of the government.... So multifarious have become corporate affairs, so many concessions and privileges have been accorded them by legislation—so many more are sought by further legislation—that their specially retained representatives are either elected to office, directly in their interests, or maintained in a perpetual lobby to serve them.[2]

The corporations had in fact cracked the code of how politics worked in America at the time and were able to have incredible influence on the entire political process because of the party bosses. Before the 20th century, political parties nominated candidates through caucuses or conventions. These events were, of course, so heavily dominated by the party bosses and their machines that it was virtually impossible to win a party's nomination if you were not the bosses' pick. And if you were the pick, it was understood that you did exactly what the bosses wanted: you served at their pleasure, not the pleasure of the people.

Suffice it to say, many times what the bosses wanted was an elected official who gave concessions to the corporations. Then everyone walked away happy, except of course the American people. La Follette continued:

The official obeys whom he serves. Nominated independently of the people, elected because there is no choice between candidates so nominated, the official feels responsibility to his master alone, and his master is the political machine of his party.... Experience has proved it almost an idle folly to attend a caucus with the hope of defeating the machine.... The citizen recognized the supremacy of the machine and abandoning the contest, the official recognizing the supremacy of the machine obeying its orders. What then have we left? It is the very life of a republic that the laws shall be made and administered by those constitutionally chosen to represent the majority. Government by the political machine is without exception the rule of the minority.[3]

La Follette concluded that day by saying,

> When legislatures will boldly repudiate their constituents and violate the pledges of their platforms, then indeed have the servants become the masters, and the people ceased to be sovereign – gone the government of equal rights and equal responsibilities, lost the jewel of constitutional liberty. Do not look to such lawmakers to restrain corporations within proper limits. Do not look to such lawmakers to equalize the burden of taxation. Do not look to such lawmakers to lift politics out of the ways of darkness.... Let us here, today, under this flag we all love, hallowed by the memory of all that has been sacrificed for it and for us, dedicate ourselves to winning back the independence of this country, to emancipating this generation and throwing off from the neck of the freemen of America, the yoke of the political machine.[4]

La Follette firmly believed that if the party bosses and their machines could be broken, then the hold of the corporations over politics would be broken as well and the will of the American people would be served. So he set out to do exactly that. Later that summer, however, his attempt to secure the Republican nomination for governor was defeated again at the convention.

In 1900, ever relentless and on his fourth try, La Follette and his Insurgents managed to beat the Stalwarts at the convention, and he became the Republican nominee for governor. He then proceeded to travel to over sixty counties across Wisconsin, spreading his gospel of reform and anti-corporatism, eventually winning the governorship of the state that fall in convincing fashion by over 100,000 votes.

On day one of his new administration in Madison, La Follette began systematically to implement his ideas for reform. Using the University of Wisconsin in Madison as an incubator for his ideas, La Follette's proposals became known as the Wisconsin Plan or Wisconsin Idea, considered by many to be one of the central pillars for the Progressive Statist movement. He called for the employment of technical experts for public service (a managerial class), direct primary nominations, railroad regulation, and tax reform (which called for the income tax and helped lead to the eventual formation of the IRS). Workers' rights were included in the reform, heavily influenced by the Prussian approach, which called for employers to care for their workers (which would be realized in the pension system). The political reform pushed by La Follette and other Progressive Statists revolved around having direct primaries, "Australian" ballots, and eventually the direct election of US senators, which would become a national issue and be enshrined in the US Constitution as the 17th Amendment.

The direct primaries allowed the rank-and-file voters to select the nominee, removing the selection process from the hands of the political bosses and the caucuses and conventions they dominated. As the voters became more active in the nominating process, the so-called Australian ballot was instituted. In the past, the parties had printed out the ballots, handing out the "party ticket" ballots to the party faithful before they entered the voting booth.

The Australian ballot, or secret ballot, was first practiced in the US in the late 1880s. The ballots were, as the name suggests, an Australian voting reform in which government entities, not partisan parties, would print the ballots and the voter would take an unfilled ballot into a voting booth and have the power of the secret ballot. In addition to direct elections, the ballot reform also undermined the party bosses' stranglehold over the voting process.

As for the direct election of US senators, La Follette had seen the previous system abused in which, as laid out by the Founders, every state was to have two US senators regardless of population. Those senators, until the 20th century, were in fact nominated by the various state legislatures, with the state houses and senates often coming up with different nominees, who were then voted on by the legislators to represent the state in DC. What the corporations, especially the railroad corporations in Wisconsin, had figured out was how to grease the process with the party bosses: get the right state legislators under party-boss control and *viola*, you now control the process of who becomes a US senator.

To deal with the corrupted process, Progressive Statists began the call for the direct election of US senators to destroy the power of the party bosses and corporations over their selection. Under La Follette and other Progressives' reform ideas, senators would now be chosen directly by the people in hopes the senators would be more accountable to the people and their state's voters than the corporations and party bosses. While it "solved" one problem, the change created another even greater one by unmooring senators from their state and accountability to the state legislatures, destroying one of the key aspects of federalism.

La Follette's Wisconsin Idea also included calls for greater regulation of the railroad corporations. He and others felt they were not bearing the burden on taxation and were of course manipulating the political system for their own gain, including at times massive bribes directly to the state legislators, as happened in 1856 when 67 percent of the state legislature was bribed with over $800,000 in railroad bonds by the La Crosse and Milwaukee Railroad Company.[5] But the greatest triumph in La Follette's mind was the eventual passage of the civil-servant law in Wisconsin. Before the passage of the civil-servant bill, those who won political office had handed the various positions in government to their friends and cronies, a patronage system in which to the political victor belong the spoils. This of course at times resulted in disastrous management of cities and states as the friends of the political victors were not necessarily qualified for the jobs handed them. In addition to creating an educated elite that would be skilled in the ways of administration, La Follette's Wisconsin Idea also made it very clear that this managerial class of experts didn't "instruct politicians so much as *replace* them" (emphasis added).[6] Again, that was the point of Progressive Statism then, and it is the point today: the real governing is to be done by the unelected educated elite.

Progressives lauded La Follette and his reforms, describing Wisconsin as a "scientific laboratory of reform.... Wisconsin is the most efficient commonwealth in the United States, a model for America just as Germany was for the world. Germany was the world's most advanced scientific state because it was the first to call in the experts, but Wisconsin was not far behind."[7] And the best part about Germany, according to the education reformer John Dewey, was that "Germany subordinated its legislature to the bureaucracy which conducted the real business of government—administration."[8]

La Follette's Wisconsin Idea would become extremely influential for the national Progressive Statist movement that began to spread across the United States in the mid-1890s. Seeking a "purification of government," the Progressive movement embraced the state not as a necessary evil but as a vehicle by which virtuous progress could be made. All of society's ills, all aspects of life, the corruption in politics, could be addressed and solved by a government run by educated civil servants: an enlightened state would manage society, to "level it out" and address social justice.

La Follette would serve as the governor of Wisconsin from 1901 to 1906, implementing much of his Wisconsin Idea, although he met strong opposition from conservative Republicans inside the state. In 1906, La Follette sought and received the appointment as a US senator from Wisconsin, serving in the US Senate from 1906 until his death in 1925. He quickly became the leader of the Progressives in the US Senate, actively campaigning for other Progressive candidates across the country and working tirelessly for Progressive Statist goals.

In 1911, La Follette provided one of the deciding votes to pass the resolution introduced by Senator Bristow of Kansas that called for amending the House resolution for direct election of senators by removing the "race rider" from the House version. The "race rider" clause, meant to "bar federal intervention in cases of racial discrimination among voters," had been a point of disagreement that, once cut, allowed the direct election of Senators to move forward.[9] That bill in turn passed the House and returned to the Senate where in May 1912, the bill was passed and then sent to the states as a proposed constitutional amendment. This became the 17th Amendment, providing for the direct election of senators.

Considered by now the national leader of Progressives, La Follette was their leading standard bearer in the 1912 presidential elections until Theodore Roosevelt, who had claimed upon leaving the White House in 1909 he would never run again, threw his hat into the ring in early 1912. Upon Roosevelt's entry, La Follette's support collapsed. Frustrated and embittered by what he saw as betrayal and Roosevelt's opportunism, he became embroiled in a bitter fight with Roosevelt, which in the end caused La Follette considerable reputational damage and standing in the Progressive movement.

Despite the setback, La Follette continued to champion the Progressive agenda in the US Senate. He was the only Republican senator to vote for the Revenue Act of 1913, which instituted the federal income tax, believing it would help Progressives achieve their goal of income redistribution. After a failed presidential run in 1924, La Follette passed away at the age of seventy, having left an indelible, and undeniably damaging, imprint on American politics.

CHAPTER FOUR

HERBERT CROLY AND HIS PROMISE OF AMERICAN LIFE

Though Herbert Croly is by far the least known of the Four Horse-men, his influence on the rise and impact of the Progressive Statist movement shouldn't be underestimated. Born to two Progressive jour-nalists in New York City in 1869 and baptized into the atheist religion of humanity,[1] Croly spent years in and out of Harvard, eventually withdrawing for the last time in 1899. Living a rather understated and wandering life of little note, he became an editor for an architectural magazine between 1900 and 1906.

It was in 1909 that Croly shot to fame in the Progressive Statist movement with the publishing of his first book, *The Promise of American Life*. While the book never became a bestseller, only moving roughly 7,500 copies in its day, it became in many ways another blueprint for the implementation of Progressive Statism because of who read it.

In his book, Croly laid out the argument for a new form of democ-racy, one focused not on protecting equal rights but rather on "bestow-ing a share of the responsibility and the benefits derived from political economic association, upon the whole community."[2] And what did that look like to Croly? Not a government existing to protect natural, inherent rights, but one that was far more proactive in ensuring certain outcomes. For that to happen, he proposed the nationalization of corporations, strong labor unions, and a strong central government.

In an attempt to rationalize this new form of "democracy," Croly attempted to fuse together what he considered the two leading philosophies of the Founding: Thomas Jefferson's ideas of democracy and Alexander Hamilton's ideas for a stronger federal government.[3] Croly's efforts, however, were nothing more than an attempt to mold those two philosophies into what he wanted by leaving out a core tenet of both Jefferson's and Hamilton's thinking: the strong, foundational belief in individual rights and the protection of those rights.

While Jefferson and Hamilton had differing views on how to achieve the best form of government, both were deeply committed to individualism and individual rights—in fact, so much so that Hamilton believed that the entire machinery of the American Republic with its separation and diffusion of power was in fact the best way to protect inherent rights, and they needn't be listed out on a piece of paper. Why did both men agree on this point? Because individual rights prevented the consolidation of power into the hands of a few, which is what the Founders were adamantly opposed to and exactly what the Progressives sought.

For Progressive Statists, a government committed to protecting natural, inherent individual rights was a government that was, of course, limited, in its size but also, in their thinking, in its scope and usefulness. To go beyond those limitations on government, to make government unlimited, individual rights must be transcended and made subordinate in the newer form of "democracy" in which the state was everything. All must be subservient to the state, all barriers of loyalty to the state removed. In fact, Croly argued in *The Promise of American Life* that parties must be done away with to achieve that end he was convinced that "partisanship itself detracted from the exclusive devotion that an individual ought to give directly to the state. When one identified as a partisan of a particular party, one could not also be a partisan of the organic whole—the state itself."[4] For Croly, the party system "demands and obtains for a party an amount of loyal service and personal sacrifice which a public-spirited democrat should lavish only on the state."[5]

Croly's vision was a concentration of power into the hands of a few to resolve any conflicts in society, the chief source of which he saw as private property. To remove the cause of conflict, he argued that the removal of property, the nationalization of corporations, and then the redistribution of it all would in fact make the country more democratic. Like every other adherent of statism, from communism to fascism, Progressive Statists were very much for either controlling or redistributing wealth and property, all in the supposed aim of creating a more just society, which is very conveniently shaped to benefit the ruling elite.

Croly, like Wilson, also believed that a ruling elite, a powerful few, should be entrusted with great power. He likewise naively thought that somehow those few would never abuse the tremendous power bestowed on them through the envisioned administrative state. Contemporary critics of Croly's believed that such an idea, if implemented, would lead to totalitarianism, fascism, and authoritarianism, which in fact it has. When it is said that the ultimate end of Progressive Statism is authoritarianism, it is not a new observation but one dating to the very beginning of the Progressive movement; its end that is now coming into full fruition in the 21st century.

In 1914, Croly continued to gain influence with the Progressive Statists by launching *The New Republic* magazine, which was seen, then as now, as the leading magazine of Progressive thought. In 1915, Croly followed up *The Promise of American Life* with *Progressive Democracy*, which focused on how the US Constitution as originally written by the Founders was in fact inconsistent with modern American democracy. This idea is central to all Progressive Statist thinking: they knew full well that their ideas of a massive administrative state, filled with a ruling elite, could never be squared with the Founders' Constitution. The Constitution and the Republic were built on the fundamental premise of protection of natural, inherent rights, via a government limited in its size and scope thanks to the separation and diffusion of power.

This is precisely why Progressive Statists, then and now, attack the Founder's Constitution: it must be either completely reimagined or delegitimized, but it cannot be left standing in its original intent for Progressive Statism to succeed. It is hard to state how emphatically, and outspoken, Progressive Statists such Wilson and Croly were in their antagonism to the Founders' belief in natural, higher law and the inherent rights that spring forth from that belief. As John Marini writes in *Unmasking the Administrative State,* "The Progressive movement... had as its fundamental purpose the destruction of the political and moral authority of the US Constitution."[6]

Croly knew full well that the entire system of the Founders had to be deconstructed if Progressives were to triumph. This is why he wrote that, in the 20th century, he perceived the Constitution to be a "living Constitution" that could be reimagined into whatever Progressive Statists wanted, something starkly different from what the Founders intended. In short, while the terms might be the same, the essence must change.

The term "living Constitution" is a central and constant one with all Progressive Statists. Originalist intent that remains consistent, instead of a moldable document, was and is the enemy for Progressives. The Founders knew their own limitations and imperfections and put in place the amendment process to address issues in the future, to further refine and better the Constitution. But their concept of a "living Constitution" is far different from the Progressive Statists, who via their ideas of a "living Constitution" envisioned reimagining the essence of almost everything from the separation of powers to the question of who governs, thereby destroying the machinery of the Republic and consolidating power into a strong central government.

Like Wilson and other Progressive Statists, Croly felt that the ultimate end of their "progress towards perfection" was "a welfare-state system patterned after that of Europe and Germany in particular."[7] The great historical irony in all of this is that the Founders had declared independence from such statist ideas, but Progressives, then and now, are intent upon returning to those ideas.

While Croly's books were never widely read, they heavily influenced men like Theodore Roosevelt, who in 1912 incorporated much of Croly's thinking into his "New Nationalism" during his run for president under the Progressive Bull Moose Party banner. Another man deeply influenced by Croly's writings was Felix Frankfurter, a leading Progressive Statist who helped engineer FDR's New Deal and later became an associate justice on the US Supreme Court. Though Croly passed away in 1930, many historians credit him as the godfather and one of the central architects to FDR's New Deal programs because of his influence on those who enacted it.

CHAPTER FIVE

THEODORE ROOSEVELT'S NEW NATIONALISM

The final horseman is the one who in many ways helped make Progressive Statism a more coherent and cohesive national movement by becoming its national standard bearer: Theodore Roosevelt. The youngest president in US History, Roosevelt was elevated to that position at the age of forty-two after the assassination of President McKinley in 1901.

A Republican for most of his political career, Roosevelt became known as the "Trust Buster" (trusts being the forerunner of monopolistic corporations) when in his first term his administration used the Sherman Anti-Trust Act to break up the Northern Securities Company, a monopoly that controlled the main railroad lines from Chicago to the Pacific Northwest. When the Supreme Court upheld his use of the Sherman Act, Roosevelt proceeded to break up other monopolies.

It was also during his first term that Roosevelt called for the formation of the Bureau of Corporations, a new government agency that was meant to gather information on corporations, especially about their monopolistic practices, and make recommendations to Congress for new regulations (this was the forerunner to the Federal

Trade Commission). His fights against monopolies helped lead to re-election in 1904. Upon winning in a landslide, he told his wife, "My dear, I am no longer a political accident."[1]

It was in his second term that Roosevelt began drifting towards Progressive Statism, with one of his signature acts being the Hepburn Act in 1906. While not much is known about the Hepburn Act today, it is considered by many to be one of the foundations of the modern-day administrative state. Using information gathered by the Bureau of Corporations, Congress passed the act, significantly expanding the Interstate Commerce Commission's jurisdiction to include the ability to set "just and reasonable" maximum railroad rates. To further that, the act empowered the ICC to examine railroad corporations' financial records, giving the government the sole discretion to decide what was just and reasonable in regard to railroad rates. The act also gave the ICC authority over a great deal of the infrastructure involved with the railroad industry, from bridges, terminals, ferries, and railroad sleeping cars to even oil pipelines.[2]

But it was only after the midterms of 1906 that Roosevelt began fully to embrace Progressive Statism. He now called for "stronger controls, not only over the railroads, but across the entire industrial economy as well. To that end, he supported legislation that would convert the Bureau of Corporations into a full-fledged regulatory agency modeled on the extensive powers he envisioned for the ICC."[3] While his ideas did not come to full fruition, Roosevelt left little doubt he was in pursuit of a statist regulatory regime, even calling for a graduated income tax and inheritance tax to fund an expanded bureaucratic state.

After leaving the White House in 1909, pledging that he would never run again for the presidency, Roosevelt became a full-throated champion of Progressive Statism. Shortly after leaving office, he traveled to Europe where he delivered a series of speeches in France and England laying out his vision for the future of American democracy (then as now, Progressives have always been attempting to cast "democracy" into whatever they say it is). It was during this time that Roosevelt was given by his close friend and supporter Learned Hand a copy of Herbert Croly's *The Promise of American Life*, whose ideas Roosevelt quickly embraced. In April 1910, Roosevelt gave a speech at the Sorbonne in Paris, "Citizenship in a Republic," in which he warned that "the doctrines of extreme individualism" in a republic were as "dangerous to a republic as those of extreme socialism."[4]

He returned from his European tour and in August of that year delivered his "New Nationalism" speech in Osawatomie, Kansas. There was now no doubt that Roosevelt's new mission in life was to become the leader of the Progressive Statist movement. In his speech, he dismissed the Founders' ideas on property rights and the notion that one has a natural, inherent right to the fruits of his labor, arguing instead that any right to property depended on whether the community felt it benefitted the whole: "The man who wrongly holds that every human right is secondary to his profit must now give way to the advocate of human welfare, who rightly maintains that every man holds his property subject to the general right of the community to regulate its use to whatever degree the public welfare may require it.... We should permit it (property) to be gained only so long as the gaining represents benefit to the community."[5]

To Roosevelt, the idea of individual rights, especially property rights, was a relic of a different time, but also based on a fundamentally wrong understanding of human nature by the Founders. Roosevelt, like many Progressives, was a believer in Darwinian evolution, which meant that the Founders' belief in imperfect, self-interested human nature was wrong and in his estimation obsolete. Because the new secular gospel of evolution taught that there was no such thing as "fixed human nature," human beings could progress beyond their selfish individualism. Roosevelt's goal was to move Americans beyond purely 'legal' justice towards a higher, more 'ethical' justice where citizens thought less about their individual rights and more about rights 'developed in duty.'"[6]

Such beliefs hearken back to Roosevelt's days as a student at Columbia University, where as a first-year law student he studied under John Burgess, a professor of law who also became the founder of political science in America. Burgess was a deep admirer of the Prussian philosopher Georg Hegel and was "especially vehement in rejecting the idea that the purpose of government was to protect the rights of the individual."[7]

While protecting the individual rights of its citizens was the entire basis for the Founders' constitutional republic, for Burgess the Founders had got it all wrong: imbued with Hegelian thought, he was convinced that the state, as it and human beings progressed towards the more rational and "just" society, should become less concerned with material things (individual property) and other individual rights and more focused on ethical and spiritual ends, as though the state could offer salvation.[8] Burgess impacted thousands of students over the decades he taught, molding and creating scores of future young Progressive evangelists, including Roosevelt, who was deeply attracted to the idea of "grafting German ideals onto the American constitutional order to make it more 'ethical,'"[9] as if somehow the Constitution, based on the clear-eyed, rational view of human nature, was unethical.

As 1912 dawned, Roosevelt, despite his claims that he would never run for president again, was now strongly considering another run at the White House. In February of that year, by now considered the national leader and voice of Progressive Statism in America (much to La Follette's chagrin), he was finally asked for a direct answer on whether he intended to run for president. Roosevelt colorfully responded with a phrase used by cowboys signaling they were ready to fight: "My hat is in the ring!"[10] What followed was a presidential election year that prominently featured all four horsemen of the Progressive apocalypse.

CHAPTER SIX

THE FULL ASSAULT ON THE REPUBLIC BEGINS

The Progressive Statist movement had begun percolating in the 1880s, built momentum in the 1890s, and started to gain real traction in the first decade of the 1900s. But if one were to point to a specific year where Progressive Statism truly arrived as a powerful national political force embraced by many, it was the presidential election of 1912, which was a seminal moment in American history. What followed was in many ways the acceptance of the administrative state as a governing philosophy by all major parties, albeit it on different levels and to varying degrees.

While in Ohio in February 1912, Roosevelt gave a speech in Columbus that left no doubt that he now truly embraced pure democracy. In his remarks, he laid out his ideas for the "weapons" that could be placed in the hands of the people to make government more accessible to the people: the direct primary, the initiative, referendum, the recall, the direct election of US senators, but even more radical, the recall of judicial decisions.[1] As Sidney Milkis writes in *Theodore Roosevelt, the Progressive Party, and the Transformation of American Democracy*, "Determined to grab the scepter of reform leadership, TR appeared to sacrifice the possibility of Republican leadership on the altar of direct rule of the people."[2]

The Republican primary of 1912 highlighted Roosevelt's obsession with becoming president again. He challenged his hand picked successor for the White House, President William Taft, in the Republican primary. A contentious and heated primary season ended at the convention in the summer of 1912. In Chicago, despite winning the popular vote in the primary, a dozen states, and hundreds of delegates, Roosevelt was denied the nomination by an alliance of convenience between the more establishment wing of the party and none other than Robert La Follette, who had dubbed Roosevelt "The Bluffer" and was determined to stop his rise.

At the convention in June, La Follette had his thirty-nine delegates vote for Taft's choice of convention chair, who narrowly won: had they voted for Roosevelt's, the convention might have in fact denied Taft the nomination. But as it was, Roosevelt's insurgency was turned back. Furious that Roosevelt had been denied the nomination, his supporters promptly bolted from the convention and walked over to Orchestra Hall in downtown Chicago. Over the next weeks and months, they formed the Progressive Party, which many know by its more popular name: the Bull Moose Party.

The Progressive Party convention was imbued with a fervent religious nature as reformers of all types, including the heretical Social Gospel "evangelicals," flocked to Roosevelt. Signing hymns, invoking Scripture, the Progressive Statists nominated Roosevelt in early August, who returned to Chicago to accept the Progressive convention's nomination, giving his "Confession of Faith" speech in which over the course of several hours he laid out his vision for the future, declaring that "The first essential of the Progressive program is the right of the people to rule.... the people themselves...are the ultimate makers of their own Constitution and where their agents differ in the interpretation of the Constitution, the people themselves should be given the chance, after full and deliberate judgement, authoritatively to settle what interpretation it is that their representatives shall thereafter adapt as binding."[3] Roosevelt closed by declaring, "We stand at Armageddon... we battle for the Lord!"[4]

Those gathered roared their approval at Roosevelt's words, waving their red banners and bandanas, which Roosevelt had blatantly swiped from the Socialist Party to be the Progressive Party's campaign symbol. As Roosevelt consolidated many different "reform movements" with some socialist overtones and a healthy dose of religion, cloaked in overtly Biblical language, many argued that he was using the Social Gospel movement to "provide religious cover for a 'frankly socialist doctrine.'" Even Eugene Debs, the Socialist Party nominee for president that year, charged Roosevelt with having "stolen the red flag of socialism."[5] Even more bizarrely, when Roosevelt finished his speech, those gathered serenaded him with the chorus of a popular spiritual: "Follow, follow, / We will follow Jesus, / Anywhere, everywhere, / We will follow on."

Only they replaced the name of Jesus with Roosevelt's.

After his acceptance speech, Roosevelt and the convention began drafting the Progressive Party platform. Aided by the Progressive journalist William Allen White and the noted Progressive social reformer Jane Addams, who had seconded Roosevelt's nomination at the convention, Roosevelt played a leading role in laying out the fundamental ideas for the party. The party "planks" would include direct primaries, popular control of the state courts in regard to question of social welfare and public policy, the direct election of senators, suffrage for women, the referendum, the initiative, social security and comprehensive social-welfare programs, conservation, and, of course, a large administrative state to make all of the Progressive Statist ideas a reality.

The Progressive Party not only stole the red banner from the Socialist Party as a bit of a wink and nod that it was presenting an alternative form of radicalism, it also swiped many of the Socialists' objectives and included them in its platform: the Progressive party plank on "Social and Industrial Justice" endorsed many of the Socialists' key concerns.[6]

By September of that year, the country was watching as four candidates criss crossed the country in what was truly the first modern presidential campaign: Woodrow Wilson, who had secured the Democratic nomination; the incumbent president, William Taft, for the Republicans; Eugene Debs for the Socialist Party; and Theodore Roosevelt of the Progressive Party. It was a presidential season that set the tone for the rest of the 20th century and even the 21st—and not just for the way the campaigns were conducted, including for the first time the ability to make recordings of candidates' speeches for wide distribution, or for the fact that for the first time direct primaries and Australian ballots became widespread in American politics.

It set the tone because ideas considered abhorrent a few short decades before became widely accepted as normal, even embraced: the Progressive Party with Roosevelt at its helm made it clear that it was fully intent on subordinating the Republic of the Founders and its Constitution to its ideas of pure democracy, rejecting natural rights for national democracy, and arguing, among many Statist ideas, that "the concentration of economic power required the creation of 'administrative machinery' to uphold economic justice."[7]

Of the four candidates, only Taft made something of a stand, albeit a weak and ineffective one, against the onslaught of Progressive Statism: "The propaganda for the satisfaction of unrest involves the promise of a millennium—a condition in which the rich are to be made reasonably poor and the poor reasonably rich, by law—we are chasing a phantom. We are holding out to those whose unrest we fear, a prospect and a dream, a vision of the impossible."[8] Wilson, while not quite as radical as Roosevelt, embraced many of the central tenets of the Progressive Party: the direct election of senators, the initiative, the referendum, the recall, and the significant expansion of national and state government, all of course, as Wilson declared, to "Empower the dignity of the democratic individual."[9]

During the 1912 campaign, Roosevelt went even further with his ideas for pure democracy, making the idea of the recall of judicial decisions a central part of his general election, even announcing that he would embrace having the recall for the president, leading the *New York Times*, which ironically was at the time one of the strongest defenders of constitutional order, to write with scathing disdain that the Progressives were "eager to remove all Constitutional limitations in the way of enacting social justice."[10]

Eugene Debs, running on pure Socialism, called for the abolition of capitalism, declaring that "It is to abolish this monstrous system and the misery and crime which flow from it in a direful and threatening stream that the Socialist party was organized and now makes its appeal to the intelligence and conscience of the people. Social reorganization is the imperative demand of this world-wide revolutionary movement."[11]

In the end, Wilson, thanks to Roosevelt's having fractured the Republican Party during the summer convention season, sailed to victory in 1912, winning 435 electoral votes and 42 percent of the popular vote in the four-man race. Roosevelt finished a strong second with 27 percent of the popular vote, which is still the best finish in a presidential election by a third-party candidate. Taft was badly beaten, winning a half million fewer votes than Roosevelt and the electoral votes of only two small states, Utah and Vermont. Debs trailed in last with only 6 percent of the vote.

While Roosevelt and the Progressive Party were denied the White House, they did receive a consolation prize: many of their stated goals were achieved when President Woodrow Wilson began immediately implementing Progressive Statist ideas, helping to enact the income tax via the Revenue Act of 1913 and signing into law the Federal Reserve Act and then the Clayton Antitrust Act in 1914, the latter of which led to the formation of the Federal Trade Commission. In the words of one commentator, "If an administrative state were to be the new guarantor of economic progress, it would need to be built. By March 1917, the end of Woodrow Wilson's first term, it was. Countless additions would later be made to the new regulatory edifice, but the 'fourth branch' of government was established."[12]

The 1912 election and Woodrow Wilson's administrations removed all doubts that the American body politic had been infected with Progressive Statism. The authoritarian ideas of a massive unelected bureaucratic state, cloaked with the lies of democracy, was no longer anathema to the people; it was welcomed with open arms and shouts of acclimation by many. Of course, what the American people at the time, as today, didn't understand was that Progressive Statism with its administrative state was going to obstruct access to their government and make it more distant, less accessible, and less accountable and in so doing, undermine the very idea of representative democracy and a democratic constitutional republic.

When everything else is pared away, what Progressive Statists have always wanted was in fact less democracy, less involvement from the people. As H. L. Mencken said of Roosevelt, "He didn't believe in democracy, he simply believed in government."[13] Of course that is true for all Progressive Statists: they supposedly champion the people with cries of direct and pure democracy, to make government more accessible and responsive to the American people.

But one cannot have both a representative democracy and an administrative state filled with a powerful, unelected, educated elite that is removed from accountability to the people, an unelected elite class that actually governs the people, a "ruling class" intentionally insulated and removed from the people. There is no way to square that circle: one must give way to the other and with Progressive Statists, the state is all. It is the Holy Grail for them that once achieved will supposedly bring a truly enlightened society. And if the ultimate end of history is reached, there really will be no more need for representative democracy.

It is very clear that Progressive Statists haven't truly believed in a democratic constitutional republic since the days of Wilson, Roosevelt, Croly, and La Follette. Of course they used the language of democracy and supposedly championed democracy, but for them and every Progressive Statist since, the democracy charade has been merely a tool, a means to an end, to achieve the administrative state. Once that state is achieved, Progressive Statists are done with real democracy; it's really no longer needed and is not just an inconvenience, but even more so an enemy and danger to the state. Over the course of the 20th century, with the administrative state becoming more and more firmly entrenched in DC, elections have become more an opiate of the masses, a maintained illusion that somehow change will happen if elections are won, or lost.

This is all a happy fiction to keep the American people numb to the reality of who actually governs them.

Consider this: If one truly believes that the state with its educated elite are in fact the perfect form of governing, why would you allow the people, the unenlightened, dirty little peasants, to disturb it with elections? Why would you ever let them disrupt "progress"? You wouldn't. You would wall it off and keep the people far away from those who are truly governing. After all, why would Progressive Statists allow threats like free and fair elections that might put new leadership into power who disagree and reject the administrative-state governing philosophy? That question must be asked, because it describes precisely where we are today in America.

CHAPTER SEVEN

LEVIATHAN IS BORN

If you boil down the essence of Progressive Statist thought, it comes to this: progress is to be achieved by the creation of a massive bureaucracy, completely separated from politics and political accountability, filled with an educated elite who are then to do the actual governing for the country. To loosely quote Wilson, this educated elite would consist of "the best boys from the best colleges," who would be trained and educated in administration and applied science from a burgeoning series of colleges and universities.

That's why many of the new universities and colleges founded in the late 1800s and early 1900s by Progressive Statists were done so for a unique reason: the explicit goal of importing Hegelian Prussian Statism into America and training a new generation of "administrators" for the administrative state. For example, Johns Hopkins, founded in 1876, was "established for the express reason of bringing the German educational model to the United States and produced several prominent Progressives, including Wilson, Dewey and Frederick Jackson Turner."[1] These new administrators would then, with as little hindrance and oversight as possible from politicians (i.e., the duly elected representatives of the people), do the actual governing and help direct the course of the nation in the most efficient way to achieve progress for all.

Efficiency became a byword for the Progressive Statists as they sought to apply it in all areas: government, manufacturing, race, gender, family. Name any aspect of life and there would be a busybody Progressive working on making it more efficient: efficient citizenship, efficient motherhood, efficient charity, efficient medicine, even efficient religion. The gospel of efficiency had legions of evangelists eager to meddle in every aspect of American life. Gone for them would be the messy, inefficient days of a pure constitutional republic with its separation of powers, its federalism, and its factions always seesawing back and forth with power, limiting the ability to consolidate power for "progress."

Of course these elements the Progressive Statists despised were features, not bugs, of a constitutional republic built to protect inherent rights and human nature from itself. But now all of that would be left behind as America entered an "enlightened age." Through the power of the administrative state and an educated elite, society could now progress: utopia on earth could be achieved through the power of applied science.

Except it was all a lie, built on a foundation of sand.

The lie revolves around one very fundamental issue. At the heart of the differences between a constitutional republic and an administrative state are polar-opposite beliefs about human nature.

The Founders of the free American Republic were optimistic realists: deeply realistic about human nature with its multitude of flaws and shortcomings, yet optimistic that they could, working with imperfect human nature, create a government that protected all of the God-given rights to life, liberty, and the pursuit of happiness. Faced with the challenge of creating a government strong and responsive enough to advance and protect these rights from foreign and domestic threats (including itself), the Founders infused the nascent Republic with transcendent values that have stood the test of time.

As such, the Founders were deeply distrustful of human nature and strongly believed that imperfect human beings should never be trusted

with consolidated power. The foundational principle in the Constitution of the separation of power inside of government is meant overtly
to weaken and limit government's power. The Founders firmly believed
in a very specific use of government: to secure every basic, natural,
inherent right via a republic built on the consent of the governed and
to take none of those rights away. But they also realized very clearly
that human beings are "no angels." In a fallen world in which many do
what they *can*, not what they *should*, there is a need for government:
boundaries to prevent and protect against the worst of human nature
while providing for the flourishing of inherent rights to life, liberty,
and the pursuit of happiness.

But within that government, to protect those natural rights given
to us by our Creator, the power of government must be diffused as
much as possible, not only in the federal government but between the
federal government and the state governments as well. Government
was meant to have a light touch in almost every aspect, present but in
the background.

However, the seismic, massive shift toward Progressive Statism
at the turn of the 20th century brought with it a rejection of that
fundamental belief. Armed with all the fervor of religious zealots,
they determined that science and an educated elite would accelerate
human progress. Frustrated by the Founders' Constitution, which
limited government and separated powers, the Progressive Statists set forth on a great expansion of the state, sure that a powerful
administrative state would solve all of society's ills. There were many
motivations for Progressives to pursue this, most of them misguided
but, in all fairness, some not, as in the case of railroad corporations
that rigged politics for their own gain. In Progressives' minds, the
state was now the provider from which the American people could
claim their rights; government was not necessarily the protector of
already-existing rights, but government would now allocate rights
as it deemed necessary for the advancement and enlightenment of

society. Now, in the hands of an educated elite, government was not something to be feared but something to be embraced.

Whereas the Founders were optimistic realists, the Progressives were utopian statists, deeply naive, willfully so, about human nature and the dangers of concentrated power. They mistakenly, including the post-millennial Social Gospel types, sought utopia in a fallen world; many of those who led the Social Gospel movement, such as Walter Rauschenbusch, believed that they could in fact, through the vehicle of the enlightened state, build the Kingdom of God on earth. All of this nonsense led Progressive Statists to work on concentrating tremendous power in the hands of a relative few. In defiance of the ages, in Progressive thinking, human nature was not inherently evil but was perfectable and could rise to a higher plane. Therefore consolidated power inside the state was good because it could "perfect" human nature.

Unelected, educated elites, armed with immense power, were to fill the envisioned administrative state, separated as much as possible from politics, elected officials, and the accountability the people's representatives brought. The walls dividing the branches of government were to be knocked down, and power consolidated in the hands of the educated elite to advance progress as efficiently as possible.

Bureaucrats in the vast administrative state were to be equipped, in theory and oftentimes in reality, with all the powers of the executive, legislative, and to a certain extent judicial branches, all in pursuit of efficiency that would lead to progress and eventually utopia: "Administrative government...demanded that the divided powers of the US government be consolidated. The Constitution's separation of powers doctrine, which, decentralized by design, was as inefficient and obsolete as was the 'planned scramble of little profiteers' in the age of consolidated industry. Efficient administration required that government, like industry, be consolidated, centralized, organized and administered."[2] In short, Progressive Statists wanted an oligarchy of an expert class, unhindered by a constitution, unbothered by representative interference, and free to do their own "enlightened" meddling with every aspect of society, supposedly for the "greater good" of bringing salvation to the dirty little peasants.

When the Progressive Statists grabbed the levers of power with the election of Woodrow Wilson in 1912, there was no more theorizing about what they could achieve: with a Progressive Statist in the White House and the Progressive philosophy dominating both Republican and Democratic parties, now was the moment of salvation for the country. In rapid succession, the Progressives in both major parties passed four constitutional amendments between 1912 and 1920 (the 16th, 17th, 18th, and 19th) while launching the Federal Reserve, the Federal Trade Commission, and numerous other agencies and government initiatives.

Because the four amendments passed during the first wave of Progressive Statism changed how the Republic operated so dramatically, consolidating even more power in the federal government, it's worth examining them in more detail.

THE 16TH AMENDMENT: THE INCOME TAX, THE REDISTRIBUTION OF WEALTH, AND FEEDING THE LEVIATHAN

The 16th Amendment further increased Congress's reach into the lives of the population by granting themselves the power to tax people's income. The amendment was ratified on February 3, 1913, and was for many Progressives their chance to redistribute wealth in the country to achieve social justice. But even more importantly, the income tax was a much larger revenue mechanism for funding the administrative state; tariffs on imports were reduced and income and corporate taxes were enacted via the Revenue Act of 1913, which was the legislative counterpart of the 16th Amendment.

Congress already had the power to levy taxes on income based upon the powers granted to them in Article I, Section II of the original Constitution. Article I, Section II states that "Representatives and direct Taxes shall be apportioned among the several states which may be included within this Union." What changed with this amendment was the disregard for apportioning such revenue to the states according to their population size. Instead, the sum was collected and used by the federal government.

If there was to be a massive administrative state, that state would have to be funded in a systematic and significant way to expand and grow it into every aspect of life; the "salvation of the people" must be funded. Once enacted, with the proverbial camel's nose under the tent, the state, the American Leviathan, became voracious: the original tax was 1 percent on those who earned over $3,000. By 1918, the top rate was up to 77 percent. Indeed, there has been a constant battle over tax rates for the entire 20th and 21st century, with of course the income tax currently providing the largest source of revenue for the federal government.

The first instance of Congress collecting an income tax actually occurred with the passage of the Revenue Act of 1861, which included a 3 percent flat-rate tax for anyone earning $800 or more. Later, following the presidential election of 1892, Democrats took both houses of Congress and the presidency under Grover Cleveland. One of their priorities was to lower tariffs, which resulted in the government needing to make up for that money elsewhere. Thus another income tax was born. This tax was also a flat-rate tax and, like the 16th amendment, was not apportioned among the states.

In 1895, the Supreme Court ruled that the income tax was unconstitutional because the tax was not apportioned to the states in a case that came to be known as *Pollock v. Farmers' Loan & Trust Co.* Fearing that the Supreme Court would strike down any further attempts at implementing an income tax, Congress refrained from passing any more legislation on the subject until 1909 when a group of Progressive Democrats and Progressive establishment Republicans collectively put forward what would become the 16th Amendment. The amendment reads as follows:

The Congress shall have power to lay and collect taxes on incomes, from whatever source derived, without apportionment among the several States, and without regard to any census or enumeration.

Or to put it another way: "The Leviathan must be fed by those it rules."

THE 17TH AMENDMENT: THE DIRECT ELECTION OF SENATORS AND THE POISON PILL OF THE REPUBLIC

If you had lived prior to 1913 and the passage of the 17th Amendment, you would not have been able to cast a ballot for your US senator unless you were an elected member of your state's legislature. This process of election was put in place by the original Constitution and had been utilized for 125 years. The Founders had intentionally formed their bicameral legislature in this way because they believed in the sovereignty of the states over any form of centralized government.

However, this form of electing senators met with obstacles in practice. There arose several instances where an impasse among state representatives to select and elect a member to the US Senate led to months-long gaps in representation. Additionally, in some states political machines, closely tied to corporations like in Wisconsin, controlled the state legislature and through them could effect the election of a puppet senator to the US Congress who would do their bidding.

In an effort to combat the problems Progressives saw, they proposed the 17th Amendment. As has been with their approach to nearly every problem we face as a country, they proposed the wrong solutions, and in this case their decision resulted in another push for centralized power. The same change had been proposed in the House of Representatives in 1826, but it did not have enough support then to carry it through both houses of Congress, let alone be ratified by three-fourths of the states. The 17th Amendment helped hollow out federalism. Senators were no longer as beholden to their states and the interests of their constituents as they had been before it was passed. But more importantly, the amendment continued to consolidate power into Washington, DC.

THE 18TH AMENDMENT: THE "WE KNOW WHAT'S BEST FOR YOU" AMENDMENT

When you're told you can't have something, human nature dictates that you only want it more. That's precisely what took place when the 18th Amendment was ratified and prohibited the manufacture, sale, and distribution of alcoholic beverages. The amendment reads as follows:

> Section 1: After one year from the ratification of this article the manufacture, sale, or transportation of intoxicating liquors within, the importation thereof into, or the exportation thereof from the United States and all territory subject to the jurisdiction thereof for beverage purposes is hereby prohibited. Section 2: The Congress and the several States shall have concurrent power to enforce this article by appropriate legislation. Section 3: This article shall be inoperative unless it shall have been ratified as an amendment to the Constitution by the legislatures of the several States, as provided in the Constitution, within seven years from the date of the submission hereof to the States by the Congress.

Why Prohibition? Because Progressives truly believed they knew what was best for society, to help the poor, unenlightened peasants along. So they decided to remove alcohol from society, to better the world. Besides the obvious disrespect for freedom of choice with their actions, Progressive Statists also hoped to diminish the party bosses and power brokers who many times used local saloons as bases for organizing their political machines.

The entire push for Prohibition became one of the most interesting political alliances in American history, allying Progressives with the Ku Klux Klan, who were also joined by the national temperance movement led by women. (Ironically, the KKK would also become strong advocates for suffrage, because they believed that women voting would empower the temperance movement.)[3]

After decades of advocacy from the temperance movement, the 18th Amendment was ratified on January 16, 1919, and was set to go into effect the following year. Almost immediately, this amendment led to a drastic increase in alcohol smuggling (also known as bootlegging), the proliferation of illegal bars or speakeasies, and an overall rise in crime throughout the decade of the 1920s until it was repealed by the 23rd Amendment in 1933.

Organized crime took hold of urban areas, prostitution and gambling were rampant, and home-brewed liquors led to the accidental deaths of thousands due to methanol poisoning from improper methods. The amendment is largely considered a complete and total failure by most historians as it led to the exact opposite of the desired result. Of course its failure did nothing to slow down the busybody Progressive Statists, who promptly upon the failure and disaster of Prohibition launched into the massive expansion of the administrative state with the enactment of the New Deal under FDR.

THE 19TH AMENDMENT: SUFFRAGE FOR WOMEN

The passage and ratification of the 19th Amendment extended the right to vote to women in state and federal elections.

The amendment reads as follows:

The right of citizens of the United States to vote shall not be denied or abridged by the United States or by any state on account of sex. Congress shall have power to enforce this article by appropriate legislation.

The amendment was ratified on August 18, 1920, following almost a century of the women's suffrage movement. The national movement for women's suffrage was launched by Elizabeth Cady Stanton and Lucretia Mott, who organized the Seneca Falls Convention in 1848.

The efforts continued in 1878 when the California senator Aaron Sargent proposed a suffrage bill, but it was rejected in 1887. Another amendment was proposed the next year, in 1888, which called for limited suffrage for women who were spinsters or widows who owned property, but this too was rejected. Following years of women's suffrage groups organizing protests, hunger strikes, and arrests, President Woodrow Wilson threw his public support behind the amendment, and it was ratified shortly thereafter.

These amendments, especially the 16th and 17th, consolidated more power in Washington, DC, and of course gave Progressive Statism the funding vehicle by which to build out the administrative state with the income tax and the Internal Revenue System. With more funding has come more growth, more agencies, more subagencies, more departments—from now until the end of time, if Progressive Statists have their way.

The vicious cycle continues as the unlimited and voracious administrative state perpetually demands more funding, and therefore more taxes, to the point now that many Americans are paying roughly half of their income in taxes. This is not a bug of the Progressive administrative state; it is a feature. The state is salvation, therefore it cannot, must not be limited, and its growth is meant to be perpetual until all aspects of life are "saved."

CHAPTER EIGHT

BUILDING A MODERN-DAY BABEL

With Woodrow Wilson's victory in the 1912 presidential race, the premise of an administrative state was accepted by many in America: there was no doubting what was being proposed after decades of Wilson, Croly, La Follette, Roosevelt, and their fellow Progressive Statists' agitations. With his inauguration, Wilson's administration established a significant and lasting beachhead for Progressives in America.

It was a triumph of Prussian Statism: the quaint notions of limited government and separation of powers conquered, the tired old ideas propounded by benighted, wig-wearing men of the 18th century retired to the history books while Progressive Statism took center stage. "We are not bound to adhere to the doctrines held by the signers of the Declaration of Independence; we are as free as they were to make and unmake governments. We are not here to worship men or a document," Wilson once declared.[1] The new "enlightenment" had begun, and by the power of the state progress would be made.

In reality, Progressive Statism and its administrative state are a modern day Babel. In the book of Genesis, the story is told in which people came together to build a great tower into the heavens so that they might be like God: through the work of their hands, by their human intellect, they would achieve transcendent perfection. The arrogance of the Progressive Statists was just as those at Babel: they raised their tower with the administrative state, firmly convinced that they could achieve the perfectibility of humanity. The new Babel is as doomed to disaster as the first was, because times may change, centuries and millennia come and go, but one thing remains constant through the ages: flawed and imperfect human nature.

Efficiency via applied science, with human progress achieved by an all-powerful state filled with an educated elite, was a religion to the Progressive Statists, who in their arrogance decided that they were better, more intelligent, more advanced, immune to base and inherently flawed human nature; where others had failed, they would succeed. It was, as C. S. Lewis describes it, "chronological snobbery," the "uncritical acceptance of the intellectual climate common to our own age and the assumption that whatever has gone out of date is on that account discredited."[2]

Progressive Statists trusted themselves implicitly which then allowed them to defy the wisdom of the ages and the Founders' view of human nature. This allowed them to smash and destroy the machinery of the Republic, which was built on the foundation of a belief in imperfect human nature.

As I wrote in *Restoring Our Republic*, the machinery of the Republic, with its separation and diffusion of power, was what many such as Alexander Hamilton and James Madison viewed as the greatest protection of individuals' basic, God-given rights: if government power was not consolidated but diffused, it would be much harder for government to abuse those God-given rights. The weaker the government power, the less the threat to rights and the greater the flourishing of freedom. That is the essence of the free American Republic, a radical notion at the time: that individual freedom and the protection of inherent natural rights are the ultimate purpose of government.

That's why Hamilton was initially adamantly opposed to an enu-merated Bill of Rights as proposed by George Mason, for fear that spelling out those rights would in fact limit how expansive they were understood to be. Better by far, in Hamilton's thinking, to build a government that would never have the strength or power to destroy rights and to enumerate the powers given to government. What was then expressly granted to government was the line drawn as to how far government might go; the rest of the rights that exist were assumed to remain vested in each individual.

An appreciation of the philosophy of decentralized constitutional government and the limitation of its powers as constructed by the Founders is central to understanding the Progressive Statists. They loathed and despised the constitutional separation of powers because it limited their ability to consolidate power to supposedly accelerate progress. In fact, in Wilson's mind, the separation of powers was a defect of the Constitution: "It is...manifestly a radical defect in our federal system that it parcels out power and confuses responsibility as it does. The main purpose of the Convention of 1787 seems to have been to accomplish this grievous mistake."[3]

Wilson appears conveniently bewildered by the exact point of the machinery of the Republic, instead arguing that the Founders' ideas of the machinery of the Republic were outdated: it was time to accept that government was "not a machine but a living thing.... Living political constitutions must be Darwinian in structure and practice.... All that progressives ask or desire is permission—in an era when 'development,' 'evolution' is the scientific word—to interpret the Constitution accord-ing to the Darwinian principle; all they ask is recognition of that fact that a nation is a living thing and not a machine."[4]

The Founders of course knew the American Republic would grow, times would change: that is why they put in place the amendment process, which was not a quick enough fix for Progressive Statists, who wanted progress *now*, who wanted the state and its consolidated powers *now* because the state was salvation and salvation must be had *now*. Tearing apart the Republic's separation of powers, which protected inherent and fundamental rights, was in the minds of the Progressive Statists the only way to solve government inefficiency. The only separation they were interested in, as clearly stated by Wilson and many other leading Progressives, was the separation of administration from the accountability of politics.

Because they trusted themselves and were motivated by a quasi-religious belief in efficiency, all barriers had to be removed to put us on the efficient path to progress. Yet the path to efficiency, flowing out of a powerful state, is actually a path to statism and ultimately authoritarianism. Central to all the various governmental philosophies and beliefs that revolve around a powerful state, be it fascism, communism, and progressivism, lies the inescapable truth: once a nation and a people begin down a path of statism, in which the state is all, the ultimate conclusion is authoritarianism.

Why? Because if one believes in the power of an administrative state filled with the enlightened and educated elite to achieve progress, eventually anyone who questions, doubts, or tries to prevent such progress is ultimately treated as an enemy to the state and progress. Dissent ultimately cannot be tolerated.

Progressive Statists knew what they were doing and yet still did it because they truly believed that they were more enlightened than the Founders. To read the writings of the Progressive Statists at the turn of the 20th century is to read the rantings of arrogant and deluded madmen. And while dangerously naive about human nature, Progressives at the turn of the 20th century must not be excused for their misguided, rampant enthusiasm for applied science in the hands of a few. They were very clear about how they viewed human rights, the power of the state, and where the balance of government should lie. They were most assuredly committed to the idea of a massive regulatory state and redistribution of property and income for "social justice" in complete and total defiance of the Founders.

In short, they knew exactly what they were doing.

Take for example Theodore Roosevelt on private property rights and his belief that no one was entitled to property unless society deemed it beneficial. Now understand that the Founders believed that, as Madison wrote, "As man is said to have a right to his property, he may be equally said to have a property in his rights."[5] In the Founders' thinking, every American had a right to actual property such as land, homes, guns, etc..

Yet they also believed that the rights inherent to every individual, the rights to life, liberty, conscience, intellectual ideas, speech, and the right to defend those rights were also property inherent to the individual. Those ideas and rights were sacrosanct: since they were endowed by a Creator to His created, what no earthly power had given, no earthly power could take away. And any earthly power that attempted to take away those rights, as the British Empire sought to do, must ultimately be resisted by force. Furthermore, to fail to defend those rights was to demean and disgrace the Creator who gave those rights.

Roosevelt, along with many of the leading Progressives, did not view the concept of rights as the Founders did. He felt that an individual's rights, from property to everything else, must be subsumed for the greater good of society. Therefore no one has any rights except those given to him by the state when considered *beneficial* for the advancement of the state and society. For Progressive Statists, ultimately, rights to anything come from the state. If one claims individual rights in defiance of state actions, it throws the proverbial monkey wrench into the gears of "efficient" government. If millions, or even tens of millions were to claim their inherent rights, it would limit the advancement of "progress." For a rational society to be achieved, in Progressive Statist thinking, it is in fact selfish and detrimental to society to claim individual rights.

Frank Goodnow, another key Progressive Statist, was, like Roosevelt, also a student of John Burgess at Columbia. He would become the first president of the American Political Science Association and eventually the president of Johns Hopkins University. It was Goodnow who really put "flesh to the bones" of Wilson's idea of administration, by engineering via administrative law a "science of administration *separated* from the limits of constitutional government" (emphasis added).[6] Goodnow, like almost every Progressive Statist, was fascinated by European political systems, particularly Germany's, where, according to him, "The rights which [an individual] possess[es] are it is believed, conferred upon him, not by his Creator, but rather by the society to which he belongs. What they are is to be determined by the legislative authority in view of the needs of society. Social expediency, rather than natural right, is thus to determine the sphere of individual freedom of action."[7]

For Goodnow and all Progressives, the ideas of natural rights, together with just associations and social compact between human beings to protect those natural rights, needed to be done away with: a belief in natural rights and the protection of them in fact limited the size and scope of the state, which is exactly what the Founders intended. So these fundamental ideas needed to be attacked, diminished, and discarded. Goodnow fleshed out this idea in his lecture "The American Conception of Liberty," where he stated, "While there is no justification in fact for this social contract theory and this doctrine of natural rights, their acceptance by thinking men did nevertheless have an important influence upon the development of thought and in that way upon the actual conditions of human life."[8]

For Goodnow, those ideas and the men who believed them were all wrong. He also included in his lecture, in true Progressive Statist thinking, his reason for why individualism based off natural rights must be done away with: efficiency. "Social efficiency probably owes more to the common realization of social duties than to the general insistence on privileges based on individual rights."[9] For Progressives, it is in fact selfish to insist on and demand individual, natural rights. Mary Parker Follett, another influential Progressive Statist at the turn of the 20th century, likewise wrote: "If my true self is the group-self, then my only rights are those which membership in a group gives me. The old idea of natural rights postulated the particularists individual; we know now that no such person exists.... Thus man can have no rights apart from society or independent of society or against society.... The truth of the whole matter is that our only concern with 'rights' is not to protect them but to create them."[10]

The theory of natural rights given by a Creator, out of which flow a republican system of government to protect those rights, was anathema to Progressive Statists because it limited them in almost every way. If government was meant to protect rights and take none of them away and was limited in its size and scope, then they could never achieve a massive administrative state. Thus, where basic rights come from had to be questioned and redefined.

It cannot be stressed strongly enough what a pivotal moment in American history and society this is: for the Founders, the very reason government existed was to protect individual, God-given, inherent rights and take none of them away. They constructed the machinery of the Republic to reflect that belief; that is the entire basis for the American Republic. The Progressive Statists rejected that aim: to have diffused power to protect individual rights was an incredible obstacle to their goals. For them the state was all, a noble force guided by the elites to achieve progress and eventually the apotheosis of mankind. To achieve that, all must be subsumed by the state, including individual rights.

Because of that view of rights, Progressives strongly advocated for redistribution and were Orwellian in their definition of property. When the early Progressives said they wanted to dismantle capitalism and eviscerate private property rights, we should believe them: they've always been socialists and anti-capitalists. Walter Rauschenbusch, the father of the Social Gospel movement in America, argued that men must overcome "their attachment to private property" and that private property rights should be removed "as an obstacle to social action" and for "socializing property."[11] Rauschenbusch was not shy about advocating "Christian socialism as a means of achieving the kingdom of God on earth."[12]

Rauschenbusch wrote in *Christianizing the Social Order* that "property rights will have to be re-socialized to bring them into accordance with our actual moral relations.... But the plain path of justice and good sense is blocked by our property rights brought down from a different past."[13] He continued: "Society has rights even in the most purely private property. Neither religion, nor ethics, nor law recognizes such a thing as absolute private property rights.... The whole institution of private property exists because it is for the public good that it shall exist. If in any particular becomes dangerous to the public welfare, it must cease."[14] He wrote towards the end of the work that "the resocializing of property is an essential part of the Christianizing of the social order."[15]

As was common among all Progressive Statists who embraced Hegel's historicism and the idea that "the state is the march of God on earth," Rauschenbusch believed that everything must be subservient to the state and the society that flowed from that almighty state. Individualism and private property had to be left behind so that America could advance to a bright and glorious future. What makes Rauschenbusch's Social Gospel even more troubling is his cloaking of statism and authoritarianism in the veneer of Christianity, as though anyone who resisted his social gospel was in fact not truly an enlightened Christian. What Rauschenbusch and other Social Gospel adherents did was elevate the state over God. But there can only be one Creator and giver of inherent rights, and it is most assuredly not the state.

Herbert Croly, coming from a more atheistic view than Rauschenbusch, arrived at the same conclusions regarding property because of his central belief, shared with Rauschenbusch, in the goodness and power of the state. He wrote that "The automatic fulfillment of the American national promise is to be abandoned precisely because the traditional American confidence in individual freedom has resulted in a morally and socially undesirable distribution of wealth."[16] He then argued that the centralized state should redistribute wealth on a national scale: "In becoming responsible for the subordination of the individual to the demand of the dominant and constructive national purpose, the American state will in effect be making itself responsible for a morally and socially desirable distribution of wealth."[17] With such ideas expressed so bluntly by a man considered to be a godfather and engineer of the Progressive Statist movement, it is foolish to ignore Croly's clearly stated goals if his dreams of an administrative state are fully and completely realized.

Other Progressives reinforced the theme of redistribution, all in the name of progress. Rauschenbusch even wanted to eliminate free markets and create a fraternal democracy that shared all property in common. This is because, like all other statists, Progressives have always believed in the collective over the individual. As Thomas Leonard writes, "For progressives, the United States was an organic, evolved, singular entity—a social organism. The social organism subordinated its constituent individuals, and its health, welfare and morals trumped the individual's rights and liberties."[18] Progressive Statists, from the very beginning, have always sought to have the state subsume individual rights, and perhaps give some back—if it is merited, in the state's mind.

CHAPTER NINE

LEVIATHAN RISES

A t the heart of Progressive Statism is the belief that the state is God
in this world. As was mentioned earlier, many of the early Progressives were either schooled in Germany or influenced by German
thought, specifically thought of Georg Hegel, considered the "father
of modern historicism and totalitarianism."[1]

Born in 1770, Hegel is best known for creating the philosophy of
"historicism," which is the belief that all philosophy is a product of
the spirit of the time, the *zeitgeist*, of the philosopher; that there is no
transcendent truth; that all truth is relative to that moment in history;
and that the whole of history is a continual march from the irrational
to the rational, a march towards progress.[2]

After teaching at various gymnasiums and the University of Heidel-
berg, Hegel eventually accepted the chair of philosophy at the University
of Berlin in 1818 and was essentially a paid apologist of Prussia's King
Frederick Wilhelm III. While in Berlin, Hegel argued for the Prussian
state and against open society. He became in many ways the leading
philosopher of Prussianism, not only because the state promoted him,
but more importantly because it promoted his ideas and infected students' minds with his beliefs via the state-controlled university system.

63

Hegel believed that "The state is the Divine Idea as it exists on earth.... We must therefore worship the state as the manifestation of the Divine on earth.... The state is the march of God through the world.... The state must be comprehended as an organism.... To the complete state belongs, essentially, consciousness and thought. The state knows what it wills.... The state...exists for its own sake.... The state is the actually existing, realized moral life."[3]

As Popper writes in *The Open Society And Its Enemies*, "Hegelianism...is an apology for Prussianism,"[4] which is to say, for Prussian Statism and totalitarianism. That was Hegel's purpose. It was what he was paid to do by the Prussian king. And in the late 19th century American Progressive Statists studying in Germany would take Hegel's propaganda, embrace it, and import it to America.

If injecting the philosophy of Hegel into a free republic founded upon the ideals of limited government sounds problematic, that's because it is: Hegel's entire career has nothing to do with advancing freedom or a free society. As a paid propagandist, he aimed at promoting and advancing authoritarian philosophy in which the state was all. In fact, Hegel wrote that "The freedom of thought, and science, can originate only in the state." If faced with subversive opinions, "The state must protect objective truth.... The state has, in general...to make up its own mind what is to be considered objective truth."[5] As in there is no higher law, no transcendent law outside of the present state. The state decides what is freedom of thought, the state decides what is truth: the state gives rights, the state can take rights, and the state decides what is truth to advance what is best for the state. As Hegel wrote, "It must be further understood that all the worth which a human being possesses—all spiritual reality, he possesses only through the state.... For Truth is the Unity of universal and subjective Will; the Universal is to be found in the state, in its laws, its universal and rational arrangements. The state is the Divine Idea as it exists on Earth."[6]

Compare that thinking to the Founders': Hegel's Prussian Statism is so dramatically different as to be antagonistic to the beliefs undergirding the Constitution. Understand that the early Progressive Statists were imbued with Hegelian thought. It was the essence of what they believed: all the talk of an immortal, omniscient Creator who supposedly created every human being in His own image and endowed them with inalienable rights was all well and good; in *realpolitik* here on earth, however, the state was God. Here the state was all and above all.

One aspect of Hegelian thought that American Progressives seized on was his belief that over the course of time, as the human mind moves from the irrational to the rational, in theory, by the end of history, humanity can become perfectly rational. As one commentator has described it, for Progressive Statists "the agenda of history is the apotheosis of man, turning man into a god."[7]

This idea of the constant, upward, linear march of history is another poisonous idea of Progressive Statism. When it comes to human nature, history is not necessarily linear. It is cyclical. Of course years come and go. Of course advances are made in technology and science. But history is not a perpetual, *upward*, linear progression in the changing and elevation of human nature. That is the central problem with Progressive Statists view of history: that human nature, with applied science and technology, will somehow progress to a higher plane. Croly even wrote that Progressive Statists' ideas of "democracy must stand or fall on the platform of possible human perfectibility."[8] This has to be stressed: the entire idea of Progressive Statists' "democracy," which is a lie in and of itself and not really democracy, is built on the foundation of possible human perfectibility.

Despite any and all attempts, some noble, others not as much, to change and advance basic human nature, the more times change, the more it remains the same. That is why throughout history, as we move forward in time, we cycle through stages as human nature plays out. We are not, and never will be, on some rising linear plane towards human perfection in this imperfect world because human nature is not perfectible. This really is another fundamental rub between Constitutional Originalists and Progressive Statists: if you reject the idea of original sin and believe that human nature is perfectible in the here and now, on this earth, you will tend to be a statist in some form. If, however, you believe that human nature, while capable of great good, is never going to reach perfection in this life, and in fact must be constrained, you tend to be a Constitutional Originalist who believes in limiting the power of government in the hands of imperfect human beings.

Building off the deeply rooted Hegelian idea that the state is the march of God on earth, that history is a linear progression from irrational to rational, the aim of politics then becomes, of course, all about progress and salvation via the state. As Ronald Pestritto writes in *America Transformed*, "Cooperation with history...thus becomes a kind of divine imperative and a test of one's faithfulness to God. Those refusing to go along with the demands of historical progress [are] therefore defying the will of God himself."[9] As is evidenced in many Progressive Statists' writings and speeches, this argument was central to their advocating for more bureaucracy, for more of an all-powerful state with less representative government: those who opposed a more authoritarian state were not only backwards, lost in another time and age, but also immoral.

John Burgess was an early adherent to Progressivism and a professor of law at Columbia's Law School between 1876 and 1912. His most important contribution during those years was the establishment of the discipline of political science, with many considering him the founder of political science in America. Burgess, who believed deeply in the Hegelian "apotheosis of man," influenced thousands upon thousands of law and political-science students, who then spread the gospel of rational perfection into government.

Burgess was joined in pushing Hegelian thought in American academia by Richard Ely, an influential professor of economics at the

University of Wisconsin between 1892 and 1925. Ely took the idea of the Hegelian "apotheosis of man" and argued that, since we need to perfect ourselves (the entire point of history), government should be used as a powerful vehicle to bolster those efforts, accelerating progress towards the rational. "God works through the state," Ely wrote, arguing that the "good Christian should be more concerned with this world, not the next."[10] Government now became the savior for society, and so needed to be more powerful, more influential, and more present in the everyday lives of citizens.

This Hegelian thought led to another significant conflict between Progressives and the Founders. On one hand, the Founders believed that human beings were given all of our natural rights by our Creator. The purpose of the free American Republic was to advance and protect all of those rights without damaging any of them. In short, *the state was for man.* That is the reason the American Revolution was fought, it is the reason the Republic was founded: it was a rejection of the divine right of kings and an embrace of a form of government that would allow for the flourishing of God-given rights; as God-given rights were given by a transcendent Creator, what no earthly power gave, no earthly power could take away. Our Republic, based on the consent of the governed as stated in the Declaration of Independence, is meant to secure basic, natural, God-given rights. It does not give those rights and cannot take any of them away. This is why the American Republic was created: to protect the individual rights of every American. That is the basic premise of the Republic.

Progressives Statists rejected that approach in its entirety.

The Progressive Statists believed that *man was for the state*, in fact subsumed by the state—like everything else, because the state was all. This has been the case throughout most of time and history: men were to be subservient to the state and serve it; the state was not there to serve man. However, the struggle for dominion between man and the state changed when the free American Republic was born. Suddenly a radical shift, like a bolt of lightning, took place in history: the Republic was constructed to protect and serve natural, inherent rights of mankind. But Progressive Statists rejected that entire premise as old, tired, and ill-informed and again flipped the equation back to man serving the state. For Progressive Statists and Hegel, this was precisely the point: in Hegelian thinking, the progress of all human government was to end up exactly like Prussian Statism, the pinnacle of all government forms, which of course meant concentrating power into the state.

Describing Hegel's philosophies, Popper wrote, "I wonder if it is possible to outdo this despicable perversion of everything that is decent; a perversion not only of reason, freedom, equality and the other ideas of open society, but also of a sincere belief in God, and even of a sincere patriotism."[11] To embrace the state is to reject a Creator because the state, instead of a necessary tool to protect basic rights and provide boundaries to allow for the flourishing of human rights, becomes the giver of all things.

While many Progressive Statists would have considered themselves religious, there was a distinct perversion of Orthodox Christianity with the Social Gospel movement, but also a growing rift between religion and the business of the everyday; one was free to have personal beliefs, but the state and its experts must be the focus, the be-all and end-all, and the giver of rights if their vision for society was to work. As Roosevelt expressed, if property or other rights were contingent on what government deemed necessary for the advancement of society, then government was the final arbiter of rights, not an Eternal Being.

CHAPTER TEN

PROGRESSIVE STATISTS AND REVISIONIST HISTORY

At the beginning of the 20th century, armed with a deep belief in Hegel's philosophy, Progressive Statists began to unwind the American Revolution and why it was fought in earnest. It was clear to Progressives that the narrative that our Founders fought to restore their inherent rights as given to them by their Creator, and then formed a constitutional republic off those beliefs, would undermine everything they hoped to achieve. Those ideas and beliefs, then, must not only be dismissed but denigrated as well, because for Progressive Statists, a "rights-based theories of government limit the state's sphere of action, thus limiting the ability of the people to implement their collective will and consequently representing something less than real democracy."[1]

According to Progressive Statists, until the enlightened Progressives arrived on the scene, the poor, benighted American people had in fact been deceived by the Founders' ideas. Of course it was all propaganda and lies to achieve what Progressives wanted, which was centralized power. But they knew the barrier of the ideas of rights-based government and separation of powers must be torn down if they were to achieve their goals. That is why Progressive Statist historians like Charles Beard and others began promoting the lie that the Revolution was fought almost exclusively for economic reasons.

Beard was one of the first to directly attack the Founders' motivations and the inspiration for the Constitution and Republic. It was deeply startling at the time but now is accepted as perfectly normal, as if it were legitimate and not Progressive propaganda. Beard argued in *An Economic Interpretation of the Constitution of the United States* that the "delegates in Philadelphia were motivated by personal economic concerns and determined to produce a document that strengthened their control of government and thus assured their continued financial success" and that, instead of being praised, the Founders should be "condemned for their reprehensible self-seeking."[2]

Beard's arguments of course are in defiance of actual history and have nothing to do with the truth of the matter: the men in Philadelphia, as noted in *Restoring Our Republic*, in fact worked against their self-interests.[3] Those gathered that summer of 1787 were some of the leading men in America. They knew they would likely become the future presidents, vice-presidents, senators, representatives, and judges. It would have been in their interest to create a form of government that benefitted them, as Beard mistakenly argues they did.

But they did not do that.

What they created was the *exact* opposite of what Beard claimed: with the machinery of the Republic and the diffusion of power, the Founders did not create a government that benefitted them as the future leaders of the country. It in reality deeply limited them and their ability to use the new government for their benefit because, unlike the Progressive Statists, they did not trust themselves. They did not trust human nature. But even more so, the Founders did not gather and conspire to form a government that benefitted their narrow economic interests. They gathered to do something never done before in the history of the world: create a rights-based republic dedicated to the radical idea of human freedom.

The central reason that the colonists even fought the Revolution was for a restoration of their rights. An interview conducted in the 19th century with the last remaining survivor of Lexington and Concord is instructive on this issue. Seeking to understand why the colonists actually fought what was considered one of the world's superpowers, the young man interviewing the veteran asked, "Why did you fight? Did you fight because of the Stamp Act?" The veteran replied, "I never saw a stamp in my life." "Well, did you fight because of the Tea Act?" "I didn't drink tea. I didn't know anybody who drank tea." "Well, did you find because you read [John] Locke and other great English philosophers and were inspired by their ideas of freedom and liberty?" "I never read them. I only read the Bible, Isaac Watts hymns, and the Catechism." The young man was clearly perplexed. He then just asked, "Why did you fight?" "I fought because we'd always governed ourselves and always meant to. And parliament and the King's ministers meant that we shouldn't."[4]

So from an actual colonist who fought the British we have a summation of why the Revolution was fought: self-governance based off inherent rights. Not economics, although the taxes of course acerbated the tensions between the colonists and England, but self-governance based upon laws springing from natural, higher law. The English colonists on the North American shores had governed themselves for almost 150 years, and now those rights were being taken away.

All of this history had to be rewritten, however, if Progressive Statists were to be successful: now the American Revolution and the documents that flowed from it would all be framed in light of economics, not rights. According to Progressive "historians," the American people had been living a lie, restrained by a government that had really been constructed for the benefit of a few elites and not for the greater population. It was now time to shed the old and come into the new where government was accessed by all and democracy could finally flourish in the hands of the American people. It was, of course, all an intentional propaganda campaign to paint the Constitution and Founders in a negative light to allow Progressives to pivot the country into their statist vision for it.

In a massive administrative state, there arises the age-old question posited by the ancient Roman poet Juvenal, "*Quis custodiet ipsos custodes*?" Which is to say, "Who guards the guards?" or, as Francis Schaeffer asked, "Who controls the controllers?"[5] In the Founders' thinking, the political process of elections allowed those running the government to be held in check, *ergo* regular elections. But not with Progressive Statists: they believed politics was the corrupting force, not human nature. They have done everything they can over the course of the last one hundred years to remove oversight and accountability for those who are truly doing the governing, because what could possibly go wrong with incredible power in the hands of a relatively few imperfect human beings? It's a dangerous naïveté that's existed over the course of most of human history, from Plato and his Guardians until now.

What makes it even more dangerous beyond the concentration of power into the hands of a few is that the entire premise of the Hegelian administrative state as implemented by Progressives is that there is no end to the state's growth: again, if it's salvation, why limit it? Now we have a massive labyrinth of a bureaucracy which, like the Blob of horror-movie fame, has a voracious appetite and grows and grows and grows even until this present day, with many questions about whom that bureaucracy is actually working to benefit.

System dynamics, the study of complex systems, can help illuminate the modern Progressive administrative state. Instead of bringing the government closer to Americans—a government of "We the People," which was really never the point—the Progressives set in motion a century of bureaucratic growth and created a system of government that reinforced itself over time, growing and becoming stronger and more entrenched. The government they created was a massive reinforcing loop, in "which one action produces a result which influences more of the same action, thus resulting in growth or decline."

One must understand that the massive Leviathan of the administrative state is the overall reinforcing loop filled with hundreds, if not thousands, of other loops; agencies, sub-agencies, departments, sub-departments, the Progressives' golden calf of the Consumer Financial Protection Bureau, offices within those various departments and agencies. Over time those reinforcing loops, if they are moving in the clockwise direction, i.e., in the growth direction, will reinforce themselves and further more reinforce the overall system: the administrative state.

Which of course ties into another fundamental idea of Progressive Statism: contrary to the idea in a constitutional republic that all governmental powers should in fact be limited, if one believes the state and its elite are the solution to all aspects of life, then the state should in fact be unlimited in its power. Why limit the solution that leads to salvation? The state then continues to grow; in fact it must grow if there is to be "progress towards perfection."

With these premises underlying the administrative state, every agency, subagency, department, every reinforcing loop of the state, must grow indefinitely. In system dynamics, with every revolution a loop not only grows stronger; it also accelerates. In many ways, reinforcing loops are like compounding interest: starting slowly, accelerating, and then exploding. This is what has been happening in this country for the last century: an unconstitutional premise was accepted, the system of the administrative state was begun under Wilson, with significant bursts of growth under FDR and LBJ, agencies were added, departments were added, the system became more robust, and then suddenly, like compounding interest, over the last decades the administrative state has exploded into unprecedented size, with unbelievable power and scope.

Many don't seem to understand this was always the point.

So what is to be done with such a system? First, the premise and legitimacy of the administrative state must be questioned: people will no longer accept something that they consider illegitimate. Then, for a reinforcing loop to stop strengthening itself, it must first be stopped.

For example, an agency's growth, in funding and staff, must be frozen. As in, funding must be completely frozen: no pay raises, no additional staff, and then cut back. Then the loop must be pushed into a counter-clockwise motion so that it can devolve itself: staff are cut, an agency is shut down, and the funding eliminated. Then more must follow. For America to return to its constitutional republican roots, all conservative leaders in DC must embrace the mantra of "defund and dismantle" until the government reaches the proper size and scope, returning us once more to a constitutional balance of power in which the bureaucrats serve the representatives of the people.

However, the reinforcing loop the Progressives put in place has not been stopped, even with Donald Trump's efforts to make cuts. It is in fact still revolving again and again and again, with every passing year, becoming stronger and more reinforced.

What the administrative state has also achieved in reality is Wood-row Wilson's vision of the "educated elite" managerial class. This class is housed in a distant capital, literally for many but also figuratively. It is far removed and insulated from the people, and really from their representatives, on purpose: the separation is entirely intentional. This is the only separation of powers that the Progressive Statists were interested in: the separation of the real governing from politics. Wilson proposed it in his *Study of Administration*. His "critical contribution to this historic change was his argument that the political and admin-istrative dimensions of government should be considered separately."[6] Goodnow then took this idea of separating politics from administration and helped engineer it into reality.

So when people wonder why the unelected bureaucrats were never meant to be accessible nor really accountable to the people and their representatives, they have failed to realize that this is exactly what the Progressive Statists wanted. Now these unelected and unaccountable bureaucrats have become a world unto themselves inside this country, even weaponizing against the people who oppose them (see Clapper,

DOJ, FBI, etc.), including even concerned parents at school board meetings who were classified as domestic terrorists due to the interest they showed in their children's education.

This managerial class of experts was to use the technical approach of applied science, of efficiency, to make the country a better place for all. Today's so-called elite's deep belief in that religion of scientism shouldn't be surprising at all; Progressive Statism all began with the idea that somehow science was salvation.

What is meant by scientism? The utter, unshakeable belief that the imperfect, finite practice of science, based on the imperfect, finite human mind, is somehow the final arbiter and the highest standard of right and wrong. Consider what science is: the study of the world around oneself, the creation of a hypotheses (an educated guess) as to why something works the way it does, the application of the guess to make predictions, the study to see if that guess was right about said prediction, and if not, another educated guess.

Science is the advancement of knowledge, but never before in human history was it considered the *perfection* of knowledge. But now it is a sort of "intellectual gospel representing scientific inquiry as itself a kind of religious calling."[7] For Progressive Statists, "science was a place of moral authority where the public spirit could find religious meaning in scientific inquiry's values of [supposed] dispassionate analysis, self-sacrifice, pursuit of truth and service to a cause greater than oneself."[8]

Yet Progressive scientism demands absolute trust and submission; faith, really, in oracles like Anthony Fauci because the supposedly enlightened elite are there for the best of the country—so no critical thought, no questions, just acceptance of the idiocracy's dogmas.

The administrative state's "elite class," with its utter commitment to and belief in its own faith system of scientism and its rightness, looks at the peasants on the outside with great disdain. What could the dirty, little, provincial peasants know on any level about anything? Because they haven't been "educated" and "credentialed," they are viewed as ignorant of what is best for the country, even what is best for themselves. Better that the peasants know their role, don't rock the boat, and let their betters guide the course of society and the government.

However, there's a problem that has developed in recent times: the American peasants won't leave behind their "beliefs and prejudices," the ideas of higher law and natural rights, covenants, contracts, and the Founders and the Constitution; they won't leave behind their belief in the legitimacy of the Constitution and its "precepts" and primacy. They have become a hindrance to the progress toward the glorious future envisioned by Progressives because they insist on "the old ways" of the Constitution and the limitation of governmental powers.

All of this also hearkens back to the days leading into the American Revolution and the English ruling elite, who, as Nick Bunker writes in *An Empire on the Edge: How Britain Came to Fight America*, considered themselves the most enlightened and erudite. That ruling class looked on the American colonies as a "sinkhole of prejudice and hatred" that stubbornly refused to leave behind its covenants and contracts.[9] Because the dirty little peasants didn't know what was best for them, the British Empire, by force, attempted to compel the colonists to "see the light," eventually viewing them as seditious insurrectionists and rebels, when in reality all the English colonists in the American colonies wanted was a restoration of their rights as Englishmen.

The American Revolution, which in actuality was more the American Restoration as Englishmen fought to have their natural rights restored and then instituted a government to protect and advance those rights, was also a defeat of a detached, arrogant ruling class who viewed natural rights as more of a suggestion than sacrosanct.

This is the real revolution taking place in this country today: Progressive Statism was, and still is, nothing less than a slow-moving coup against the Founders' Republic: a complete reshaping, dramatic undoing of the Republic, quietly, behind the scenes, with many Republicans either ignorantly or willingly advancing or accepting the premise of it all. The Republic is based on the consent of the governed—and we do not consent. Our silence, however, is seen as consent, and people are silent because they do not know what is actually taking place inside our government—but then again, how could they? It's not as though they're being taught real history of the Republic in government schools; rather, the corporate propagandists and state stenographers are daily doing their best to advance the state and its elite. On every front the American people are being given the "party line" to reinforce the worldview of Progressivism. What's surprising in the 21st century is that so many Americans, despite the best efforts of the Progressive Statists, still believe in the legitimacy of the Constitution and question the state.

There is a reason Progressives have always targeted the Founders. It didn't just start with fallacies like the 1619 Project and other leftist narratives in the last few decades. Revisionist history is central to the Progressive Statists because of a fundamental incongruency with their proposals. They fully understood that a centralized administrative state was the polar opposite of what the Founders envisioned: for them, government was a necessary evil in a fallen world. Again, the Founders' conundrum was how to create a government that would have the ability to provide order and yet advance and promote God-given rights while taking none of them away. That was the central thesis to their ideas: checks and balances upon government to protect inherent rights.

But that was a real problem for Progressives, who understood why the system of checks and balances and separation of powers would prove so problematic: it was based upon the belief of individual natural rights and formulated with a very deep distrust of powerful, centralized government. The Founders had just won their independence from the crushing tyranny of England which sought to remove their rights. They had no interest at all in creating another powerful state but instead sought a government that protected and advanced individual rights.

But Progressives believed strongly that, within the administrative state as a "social organism...subsuming corporate and natural persons alike"[10] there is no real place for the individual and his or her rights; these would only get in the way of the greater good. Therefore, any idea of inherent, God-given, individual rights, and more importantly a government inspired by and built on the belief in those rights, must be done away with.

This is why Beard and other Progressive "historians" began the narrative that the American Revolution wasn't fought over individual rights but for economic reasons. For Progressives to succeed, they needed to reframe the argument about why and how America was founded in the first place: first it was economics, now it's slavery, but every attack has the same intent of destroying the real founding of the country. Thus the revisionist history, in defiance of the Founders' very words, as to why the colonists fought the Revolution, why they declared independence, and why they constructed the machinery of the Republic like they did.

This is exactly why the Progressive Statists' war against the Founders continues to this day: if you can delegitimize the Founders and their motives for independence, everything about the American Republic begins to unravel. This is why the Progressive Statists are so hell-bent on framing and then dismissing the Founders as old white, slave-owning, misogynistic racists who fought the Revolution for purely economic reasons. If you delegitimize the Founders, it stands to reason you then can delegitimize their founding documents: if the Founders are illegitimate, how can their ideas be legitimate? How can any of their documents, the Declaration of Independence, the Constitution, the Bill of Rights, be legitimate? If Progressives can fully succeed in this delegitimizing of the Founders writ large, then anything that springs forth from those documents will be seen as illegitimate.

If everything can be erased, if you can destroy and remove the old order, your revolution will succeed. You can then have a blank slate to begin a brave new order. What has prevented this from happening in totality is that even in the midst of the rise of the administrative state, it still lacks the legitimacy of the Constitution in the eyes of the American people.[11]

Legitimate or not in the eyes of the American people, the reality is that we are most assuredly governed by an administrative state. Out of that mentality and approach arises the so-called "deep state." It is in fact inevitable and is the actual goal. If you view, or define, the deep state as a system of powerful, unelected bureaucrats who think they decide, that they govern, on all things more so than any elected official, including the president of the United States, that is in fact the stated goal of Progressive Statists from the genesis of their movement. Furthermore, if you believe in the rightness of those same bureaucrats, you are then in many ways obligated to defend them and their bureaucratic state against all perceived threats.

If you were to take Wilson at his words that politics corrupts the process, according to that philosophy of "governing," you would be almost morally obligated and required to resist the "taint" of politicians "meddling." It then becomes a question of "whose side are you on?" That's why many times we see the administrative state actors working in concert with Democrats while resisting or even attacking Republicans.

If you believe the state is central to progress, you must make it an all-powerful entity. It becomes massive, sprawling, and eventually abusive. Even more so, if that state is central to progress and to a "great and glorious future," those who staff it eventually become the absolute arbiters of what is right and wrong for the country. Anyone who fights the administrative state, hinders it, slows it, delays its progress, and furthermore rejects and dismisses the "Sages of Statism" whenever they seek "enlightened progress" is thus the enemy of progress, an "unbeliever." There's no debate, no discussion, no dialogue: submit and comply or else. It's not too far a leap to then say those who are meddling with progress are in facts enemies, ergo enemies of "democracy" and "semi-fascists" who are a threat.

So why have forces such as the administrative state, the corporate propagandists, Big Tech, and the Democrat Party all arrayed themselves on one side and become a unified force against Republicans, America First, and quite frankly many of the American people? There's no real grand conspiracy happening, no smokey backroom plots being hashed out, no "need for collusion or a plot. All that is needed is that the world view of the elite and the world view of the central news media coincide."[12] It's all in plain sight: the leaders of those forces all went to the same indoctrination centers and were imbued with the same belief system.

Simply pull the thread to understand the absolute damage the indoctrination centers of higher learning having inflicted on this country and how they've led to groupthink, which really was always the purpose of Progressives and their ideas of "education." Croly even admitted that this is exactly the point of the Progressive education system: "20th century democracy believes that the community has certain positive ends to achieve, and if they are to be achieved, the community must control the education of the young."[13] It's not the individual parents who should control the education of the young; they might actually insist on teaching their children about higher law, natural rights, and all the other problematic ideas that would hinder the state. No, if all was to be an efficient path to progress, the community must educate the youth with the "right" ideas.

Students, now having been indoctrinated in Progressive Statist ideas from elementary school though high school and into college, are unfamiliar with or even taught to hate the original intent of the Founders' Constitution and its Bill of Rights. Steeped in the belief that the administrative state is the giver and arbiter of rights, with no real concept or appreciation of the idea of natural rights, they then leave their safe spaces and go into the larger world.

Miraculously, somehow, even after decades and decades of these bastions of indoctrination existing, the greater world doesn't completely resemble the dynamics of the colleges and universities. But these indoctrinated generations, now fully invested in the rightness of their ideas, begin working at places like Google, Twitter, and Facebook. Others enter government; others, the corporate propagandist ranks.

Suddenly, as if overnight—although of course, like the reinforcing loops discussed earlier, the events were actually set in motion a century ago and are just now exploding into view—you end up with senior executives from Big Tech meeting with senior officials of DHS to discuss the censoring of the American people via what amounts to a Ministry of Truth. They claim this all serves to "protect democracy" and combat "misinformation," while the corporate propagandists keep pumping and amplifying the Approved Narrative.

Suddenly, the free flow of information, ideas, and speech is severely restricted, if it even exists. Algorithms are potentially, probably, manipulated to promote candidates and leaders with the "right ideas." Narratives considered helpful to the state are promoted. Narratives considered damaging, simply because they're even mentioned, are suppressed. When indoctrinated Big Tech folks jump in bed with indoctrinated big government types, they give birth to Big Brother: a full-on, *Nineteen Eighty-Four*–style world run by bureaucrats who of course, as a cherry on top of their authoritarian groupthink, are fully convinced of their rightness.

CHAPTER ELEVEN

WHY GOVERN WHEN YOU CAN JUST WATCH?

U nderlying the history of American government for most of the 20th century is a dynamic that is little discussed: the slow, inexorable transfer of legitimate governance of this nation from the duly elected members of Congress to the unelected bureaucrats of the administrative state, to unelected bureaucrats' edicts and statutes instead of laws passed by We the People's representatives. This process, sadly, was many times of the legislative branch's own choosing. Over the course of the 20th century until today, Congress has devolved from actually governing as the people's representatives to managing or overseeing the administrative state's actual governance of the country. Congress now barely provides or enforces any real oversight, in many ways defending administrative-state actors and behaving more as the tax collectors or middlemen for the state.

After the first wave of the Progressives, from 1895 to 1920, the growth of the administrative state slowed. There were still agencies and departments added, but the administrations of Coolidge and Hoover didn't continue the wholesale regime-change of Wilson and the other Progressive Statists. You might even say there was a pause in the revolution. But with the 1932 election of Franklin Delano Roosevelt, the nephew of Theodore Roosevelt, that revolution was renewed and the administrative state began another era of major and rapid expansion.

After taking office in 1933, President Roosevelt's second wave of Progressive Statism accelerated rapidly as he swiftly delivered on his promises made on the campaign trail. Using the Great Depression as the excuse to expand the state (never let a crisis go to waste), Roosevelt initiated a series of all-encompassing projects and agencies that Progressive Statists had always wanted and termed it the New Deal. These programs included the Civilian Conservation Corps (CCC), which created jobs for unemployed people to build parks, trails, and roads across the nation, and the Works Progress Administration (WPA), which was the largest of the organizations created under the umbrella of the New Deal.

Roosevelt also began the Federal Housing Administration (FHA), which regulated housing conditions and mortgages; the Federal Deposit Insurance Corporation (FDIC), which served to insure deposits made to banks and restore trust in the financial system among the American people; the Federal Communications Commission (FCC), which regulated communications across many mediums; the Social Security Act; and far more.

These work projects built lasting structures such as the Hoover Dam, the Bay Bridge, and the Lincoln Tunnel. Many of these organizations, programs, and policies were supposed to address a short-term national need such as staggering unemployment, loss of housing, or capital and food scarcity, all of which were triggered by the Great Depression. Yet to this day many of those New Deal entities still exist, from Social Security to the FDIC to the FCC, proving once again that once something is started by the government, it doesn't die; like a vampire, it lives on forever. But even more importantly, these decisions continued the trend of state expansion, fundamentally changed the size and scope of the

US government, and shifted power away from the people and into the hands of unelected bureaucrats that really aren't beholden to anyone.

Perhaps one of the most critical acts regarding the expansion of the administrative state came during the last year of FDR's first term in the White House, when he tasked Louis Brownlow to come up with a plan for the entire reorganization of the executive branch. Brownlow, a journalist and then academic who was appointed as commissioner of DC by Woodrow Wilson, was a typical Progressive Statist who'd studied European models of government and thought it would be wonderful to import that type of governing into the United States.

Brownlow formed the Committee on Administrative Management (now more commonly known as the Brownlow Committee) and spent nearly a year putting together a report on how to reorganize the executive branch. One of Brownlow's top recommendations to FDR was to move the Bureau of Budget (which is the Office of Management and Budget today) out of Treasury and into the White House and then empower the Bureau to run the executive branch. Brownlow's recommendations became the framework for the Reorganization Act of 1939, and the Bureau of Budget was moved into the executive branch. The White House staff grew from dozens to more than eight hundred in no time, and over the years, presidents delegated more and more authority to the bureau, which became the OMB in 1970. Today, much of the president's governing is effectively done by OMB bureaucrats, who claim the imprimatur of the president and White House to tell the other departments and agencies inside the executive branch what to do. With the Reorganization Act of 1939, the administrative state became a far more permanent reality for the United States.

After a short interlude, with something of a pause on the growth of the administrative state under Truman, Eisenhower, and Kennedy, came the administration of Lyndon B. Johnson and the Third Wave of Progressive Statism. Following the assassination of President Kennedy and the impromptu swearing in to the presidency of someone poles apart in the person of Vice President Johnson, the American people were reeling after the unexpected fall of Camelot. It was into this environment that Johnson introduced his agenda, later to be known as the "Great Society," a mere few months into his presidency. The plan he unveiled in his speech in May 1964 entailed the largest leap in the size and scope of the American Leviathan in regards to social-reform plans.

In describing his plan, Johnson stated that:

> The Great Society rests on abundance and liberty for all. It demands an end to poverty and racial injustice, to which we are totally committed in our time. But that is just the beginning. The Great Society is a place where every child can find knowledge to enrich his mind and to enlarge his talents. It is a place where leisure is a welcome chance to build and reflect, not a feared cause of boredom and restlessness. It is a place where the city of man serves not only the needs of the body and the demands of commerce but the desire for beauty and the hunger for community.[1]

One element of his plan was to declare a "war on poverty" through the formation of the Office of Economic Opportunity, an effort to provide opportunities for developing skills, finding jobs, and increasing levels of education for those struggling to provide for themselves and their families. Medicare and Medicaid were passed under the Johnson administration, after Kennedy had promised them on the campaign trail but was unable to see the legislation through both houses of Congress. Additional support was provided for educational reform, urban development, environmental protections, and the arts.

Though many conservatives understand the need for society to have a "safety net" for the poor and needy, we differ in our approach from Progressive Statists. Government overreach and legislating programs that extend the need for taxpayer dollars to care for the less fortunate are agenda items that those on the Left consider to be their first and best course of action as well as, quite frankly, a long-term solution, though in fact it does not solve the problem.

For FDR, LBJ, and every other Progressive Statist, the state was the solution and salvation. By the 1970s, after three absolute Progressive sledgehammers to the Republic in a span of just over fifty years with the Wilson, Roosevelt, and Johnson administrations, many people no longer questioned whether the government should be involved in solving the problems that arose in the nation. Rather, the only question was how should government intervene and what the state's solutions were. In other words, the purpose of the government as viewed by the people shifted to an ever-increasing entity that was and should be involved in nearly every piece of the population's lives, from issuing them a social-security number at birth to taxing their estates when they passed.

What's forgotten in all of this is the obvious: the so-called educated elite bureaucrats filling the massive, sprawling Leviathan of the administrative state do not truly represent the people. They were never elected by the people to represent them, and there is no real connection to the people; in fact the people are reduced to numbers, statistics, just pieces of a puzzle as true humanity and individualism are left behind and efficiency is pursued. What makes it very problematic is that many of these bureaucrats were not elected or appointed by the people or the people's elected representatives, nor are they really accountable to the people. One could even say they are barely accountable to the supposed people's representatives. With every passing year, it is a more tenuous accountability.

These "educated elite" represent the interests of the state first, which are really their own; the people's interests are an afterthought, if even that. All of the rhetoric and platitudes about doing what is best for the country and the American people are a veneer to gloss over the truth that in fact the state and its "educated elite" are there to do what's best for the state and themselves. They consider the people, the businesses, all aspects of American life to in fact be parts of the whole state, to be subsumed and used for the state. When one grasps this concept, much of the last few decades makes perfect sense. In fact, much of American government and its actions in the 20th century come into focus.

And in the face of this massive transfer of power, what have the people's representatives done over the decades as the administrative state has grown in size, spending, and scope? For the most part, in reality, despite Republicans' wailing about big government and national debt and all the other platitudes, both parties have helped fund and transfer power to the state and have accepted the premise that the unconstitutional administrative state and its unelected bureaucrats are somehow legitimate inside of a constitutional republican form of government.

The beginning of the end of true representative government began with the First Wave of Progressive Statism (1895–1920) in that the entire proposition that an unelected, educated elite should be guiding the country was accepted and built out from there. It continued with the Second Wave (FDR's New Deal Era of 1932–45) and then the Third Wave of LBJ's Great Society (1963–69). Over those decades, the transition of power and governing took place as elected legislators slowly, but many times willingly, handed over their duties and obligations to unelected and unaccountable bureaucrats.

Some might resent that, but it is the truth. Every piece of empirical data shows this. Our representatives in government have abdicated their roles as the stewards and guardians of the American people's money and interests. Now they simply act as middlemen, allocating taxpayer money from the people to fund the state to advance the state. Ken Masugi argues convincingly in *Unmasking the Administrative State* that after LBJ's Great Society, "Congress lost the will to legislate and became facilitators of the administrative state."[2]

If one were to ask what was the real pivot point for Congress's surrender to the idea of the administrative state, the answer would be, according to John Marini, between the years of 1968 and 1978. In that decade,

Congress passed more regulatory legislation than it had done in the whole prior history of the nation. It created new agencies, such as the Environmental Protection Agency, Occupational Safety and Health Administration, and the Consumer Product Safety Commission to administer those laws. It required the wholesale delegation of lawmaking power to those newly created administrative and regulatory bodies, whose authority was dependent on technical, or rational, knowledge.[3]

CHEVRON DOCTRINE

What took that delegation of lawmaking power to administrative and regulatory bodies even further was a Supreme Court case in 1984, *Chevron U.S.A., Inc. v. Natural Resources Defense Council, Inc.* The case itself revolved around a provision of the 1970 Clean Air Act, which

> required states that had not yet achieved national air quality standards to establish a permit program regulating new or modified major stationary sources of air pollution, such as manufacturing plants. The Environmental Protection Agency (EPA) passed a regulation under the Act that allows states to treat all pollution-emitting devices in the same industrial grouping as though they were a single "bubble." Using this bubble provision, plants may install or modify one piece of equipment without needing a permit if the alteration does not increase the total emissions of the plant.[4]

But several environmental groups, including the Natural Resources Defense Council (NRDC), felt the EPA's bubble provision was contrary to the Clean Air Act. When they challenged it in the courts, the US Court of Appeals for the DC Circuit set aside bubble regulation as "inappropriate for a program enacted to improve air quality."[5] But the NRDC appealed to the Supreme Court, and what resulted was a unanimous decision that is considered a seminal case in administrative law. With the *Chevron* case, the Supreme Court decided that where there was ambiguity regarding any laws passed by Congress, the courts should defer any decisions regarding the actual implementation of the law to the relevant agency. This decision is the basis for the Chevron Doctrine, also referred to as Chevron Deference, in which the courts defer to the various agencies in regards to how statues or laws are to be applied to society in general. In short, when Congress "frames out" specific laws, there can be legal challenges as to what they look like in reality, in which cases the courts defer to the bureaucrats inside the various agencies to interpret how the laws should be enacted.

There are a whole host of issues with this entire concept. And while some argue that over the years the Supreme Court has largely ignored the *Chevron* precedent and that it's no longer an important framework for making decisions, the standing principle of *Chevron* is deference to unelected "experts" and their statutes, which is really placing lawmaking in their hands: "Although administrative rules are not laws, many of them give effect to binding statutes, and are themselves considered binding under section 553 of the Administrative Procedure Act, and in reality have the binding effect of laws."[6]

That reality essentially puts some of the legislative role into the executive branch, where most of the agencies reside, undermining the constitutional separation of powers. However, that is not the only problematic aspect of Chevron: *it is* also biased in favor of the government being right. One of the other "costs of deference, in contrast, is that it systematizes biased judgement in violation of the Fifth Amendment's guarantee of due process. . . . this makes the *Chevron* slant all the more remarkable and worrisome. It is institutionally declared and thus systematic precommitment in favor of the government."[7] This of course not only undermines American citizens' fundamental rights, but also calls into question whether there is an independent judiciary—another important aspect of the separation of powers—or whether the judiciary is at times "captured" by the executive via *Chevron*.

In other words, *Chevron* deference, with its systematic bias against the Article III branch, the judiciary, in favor of the Article II branch, the executive, where most of the administrative state resides, circumvents or undermines the Article I branch, the legislative, in many ways consolidating the three into one in the process—all while denying the American people the due process, a fair process, they're supposedly guaranteed by the Constitution.

The entire arrangement calls into question the spirit of the separation of powers and the truly independent nature of the judicial branch. We take for granted the idea of the three branches of government, that of course there has always been and always will be an independent judiciary. But ask yourself, why is there one in the Constitution? The answer is that it was a fundamental issue for the colonists in pre-Revolutionary and then post-Revolutionary America. Having been abused by judges that deferred to royal governors and the Crown, in many ways rubber-stamping the executive edicts, the Founders were determined to have a legal system that was independent of the executive:

> After independence from Britain, judges in the United States were independent from any deference to executive power. No longer tools of the executive, judges in the United States enjoyed a separate governmental power.... Judges now, however, defer to the executive's judgment of the law and thereby shift their judicial power back toward the executive. It is as if the worst of the seventeenth century has returned to life, for in giving up their own judgment and relying on the executive's judgment, the judges make their judicial power a part of the executive power... in deferring to the judgment of the executive about what the law is, judges alter the real structure of government, shifting the judicial power back into the executive.[8]

Again, the one aspect that the Progressive Statists truly hated about the Republic was the separation of powers. They have been seeking to undo it, and really the reasons for which the American Revolution was fought and the Republic founded, from the very beginning. What's staggering is when supposed conservatives go along with their attempts to hollow out the Republic, as some have done with *Chevron* for "Judicial deference to administrative interpretation is...very dangerous.... it restructures the government by shifting judicial power back into executive power; and, last but not least, it compromises the essential role of judges as independent arbiters between the government and the people, thereby undermining the very legitimacy of government."[9]

This is why *Chevron* should be abandoned. It corrupts the separation of powers and undermines the legislative branch. While it has been shuffled off to the side many times as a framework for decisions since 1984, it should be overturned on constitutional principles; it has nothing to do with the Constitution, and it legitimizes an administrative state that is unconstitutional.

WHERE WE ARE TODAY

The transfer of governing from the legislative to the executive branch continues to this very day. Congress passes four-thousand-page bills, or even 5,593-page bills, as it did with the Consolidated Appropriations Act in 2021. Many times, members of Congress do not read the bills in their entirety because there is simply no time to read them. But now that doesn't even matter, because they're not the ones actually governing: they're just useful middlemen, a pass-through by which money is apportioned to the various parts of the administrative state, which then takes these massive bills, parses through them, and, using what is really consolidated power of executive, legislative, and judicial powers, decides how to put meat on the bones of the bills, i.e., what it actually looks like to govern.

If one thought this broken process is insane and preposterous, with unelected bureaucrats, many faceless, governing the American people, one would be correct. *But it is also the precise goal of what Wilson and every other Progressive Statist wanted.* The erection of the administrative state was for them the perfect and rational state; it signaled the "end of history." It was also meant to invade every aspect of every citizen's life, in the name of progress and salvation for all humanity—the apotheosis of humanity.

Americans shouldn't be amazed at the regulatory excesses they face today, whether over gas stoves or fossil fuels or water usage or vaccine mandates or every other issue the supposed elites are attempting to compel change on. What should surprise us is that this hasn't happened sooner in the rise of the administrative state, because this authoritarianism in every aspect of life is exactly the point. People should be troubled by what is happening in the United States, but it won't be a mystery if one has read the works of Progressive Statists. The truly amazing part about all of this is that there wasn't a total collapse of freedom years ago.

Our Republic, built off the fundamental understandings of human nature and inherent rights, always intended a constitutional form of government to be limited in size and scope to provide for the "bounds of ordered liberty"; regulation would have a light touch, allowing the widest amount of space within which human freedom could flourish. It was also meant to protect humanity from the worst impulses of imperfect human nature. Never trust imperfect human beings with consolidated power. Allow freedom to flourish. Allow human beings to pursue their God-given talents while limiting as much as possible of the worst traits of humanity.

In an administrative state, however, government is not meant to be limited at all: if the state filled with an educated elite is guiding society in the upward climb to perfection, it is producing humanity's salvation. And if you believe that and accept it as valid, there should be no limiting of the size or scope of government, because who would want to limit salvation? Only an unenlightened troglodyte would. This is why there is always an imperious, arrogant righteousness with Progressive Statists: what they are really pursuing is enlightened perfection, and those who resist are fools, living in the dark ages, resisting the rise of humanity, and really limiting all of society by fighting the Oracles of Progress. They must either submit or be ostracized from society. Either way, you end up where we are today, having regressed to a mentality of *you will, because we say so—and if you don't, we will force you to.*

The result is little unelected dictators in every department, agency, and subagency, dictating to the American people how they should live their lives. There has never been real consent to these dictates or decrees.

And yet here we are.

This is again one of the great ironies of American government today: there is no one with any real power representing the American people's interests inside of government. Donald Trump attempted to be that voice. We all know what happened to him for having the temerity to suggest the American government, founded of, by, and for the American people, should indeed be advancing the American people's interests first and last in all things. On the whole, however, in recent history there haven't been any real voices with real power who have in their actions promoted the American people.

To be fair, there have been voices in Congress throughout the years who have done their best to fight for the people, but the weight of political power, the leadership of both parties in both chambers of Congress, has not. This means the people don't really have strong, meaningful advocates inside the government they fund: a government supposedly of the people, funded by the people, is not for the people. It's for the state and the stewards of the state. The people are now just the ruling class's ATMs.

Yet this entire scenario suits many people just fine, especially those in Washington, DC, and all who benefit from that system. The logical conclusion is this: if unelected bureaucrats are really managing most of the business of government, and not much truly changes between administrations whether they be Republican or Democrat, representative democracy is in fact done. Progressive Statists and all who have accepted the legitimacy of the administrative state are in fact done with democracy, with giving the people voice to self-govern.

To further the point that true representative democracy is dead in the United States, we can refer back to Wilson's ideas that elected representatives should have very little, if any, real oversight over administrators, as well as to the other Progressive Statists who praised German legislatures in the 19th century for handing over the real business of governing to bureaucrats. According to Wilson, the seamy influence of politics would corrupt the process of progress in the hands of the educated elite, who would be driven by nothing but noble purposes.

In our constitutional republic as envisioned by the Founders, all power flows from the American people to their duly elected representatives, whom they delegate authority to and empower with money and power to construct a government that advances and protects the people and their interests. One of the fundamental aspects of the administrative state is that somehow the power delegated to the people's elected representatives should then be, must be, *re-delegated* to the educated elite to do the real governing. Except that is wildly unconstitutional.

In *The Administrative State Threat*, Philip Hamburger writes:

Administrative lawmaking is often justified as delegated power—as if Congress could divest itself of the power people had delegated to it. The Constitution, however, expressly bars any sub-delegation.... How then does the Constitution bar congressional sub-delegation? The answer comes in the Constitution's first substantive word. The document begins: '*All* legislative powers herein granted shall be vested in Congress...' If all legislative powers are to be vested in Congress, they cannot be elsewhere. If the grant were merely

permissive, not exclusive, there would be no reason for the word
All. That word bars sub-delegation.[10]

But to Progressive Statists, this is all wrong: from Hegel to Wilson
and for every other Progressive Statist, legislative power must in fact
be delegated from the politically elected representatives to the educated
elite. The failure to do so, in their thinking, is the basis for many of the
ills of society: the dirty little peasants or their political representatives
shouldn't be anywhere near the real power. Our betters should be in
charge so that progress can be made towards a great and glorious future.
Allowing the peasants and their representatives to be involved, to
muddy the waters, and to ask questions is to retard and slow progress.

It is time, after a failed experiment in defiance of the Constitution
and really the reality of human nature, for America First Republicans
to reject the premise: in no way is an administrative state constitutional.
It never was and it never will be. It is a statist, undemocratic form of
governance founded in Hegelian authoritarian and totalitarian thinking
that has nothing to do with the Founders' vision for this country. It is
illegitimate and therefore must be destroyed, subagency by subagency,
department by department, until it is dismantled and put back into a
proper role: subservient to and beneath the representatives of the people.

This is *The Thing*. Nothing else matters: until the administrative
state, the deep state, and the surveillance state (mostly the same) are
forcefully confronted and dismantled, everything else is pointless. This
is why the right Republicans must gain political power in DC: not to
manage the state, not to repurpose the state, but to fundamentally
change it, break it apart, and devolve it. That goal is the sole reason for
the next generation of Republican leadership to achieve political power.

The first thing Republicans and conservatives of all stripes should
start doing is refusing to fund the administrative state blindly. There
must be a commitment to broad and deep cuts in government spending, including hiring freezes for all federal agencies, with perhaps some

exceptions for defense. But there must also be a commitment and return to legislating, which could start by not passing five-thousand-page bills for the administrators to interpret according to how they want to govern.

One of the solutions in transferring legislative power back to the Article I branch, where it belongs, would be to significantly downsize the executive branch and its administrative state—which everyone knows isn't that accountable to the head executive anyways—and take some of those resources and expand the permanent committee staff inside of Congress. This would allow the legislative branch to have more bandwidth in dealing with complex issues while returning the legislative process fully to the proper constitutional branch. The committee staff, the technical experts on subject matter, would be directly accountable to the duly elected legislators.

One of the basic principles of the administrative state is to consolidate power, not diffuse it. What has been done over the last century is to hollow out the separation of powers by consolidating legislative, executive, and judicial power into administrators' hands. If you put all three powers into the hands of one, *viola*, you have efficient authoritarianism. As others have said, "the administrative state is the modern face of tyranny."[11]

CHAPTER TWELVE

WHEN FALSE GODS
RING HOLLOW

The administrative state is built off the idea that society is best governed by the experts. But what does it mean to be an expert? Who decides what an expert is? Underlying those questions are even more questions: what do words mean, and what is "true"? What are "facts"? It's become increasingly obvious in current times that Progressive Statists define words very differently to craft a narrative in their pursuit of power. It's also clear that they are determined to manipulate words and "facts," to even change their definitions, to achieve validity as the "experts" then use these new terms. They even want to redefine truth into a subjective "your truth, my truth" discussion, which is absurd: by its very nature, if one believes there is truth, it is absolute and objective by definition. To discuss truth in the subjective is to say there is no truth at all.

Terms and who defines them have always been a focus of statists. Many on the Left today define the rule of law as whatever they say it is, depending on their political opponents, while most on the right consider it to mean the equal application of the law.

But even more so than the changing of terms, leftists have attempted to make themselves the final arbiters of definitions, much like King

George III did in the early days of the American Revolution when he declared, "I wish nothing but good. Therefore, anyone who disagrees with me is a traitor and a scoundrel."[1] Authoritarians always seek to define terms and then compel submission from anyone who disagrees with them over what their arbitrary definitions are, all of which are meant to help them achieve their own absolutist goals. It is an artifice they've used for centuries. We must reject their games: if we continue to allow them to redefine terms, we will lose.

It reminds one of the scene from *Through the Looking-Glass* when Alice encounters Humpty Dumpty. After a back-and-forth over days in the year, the two devolve into a disagreement over the definition of words:

> I don't know what you mean by 'glory,' Alice said.
>
> Humpty Dumpty smiled contemptuously. 'Of course you don't—till I tell you. I meant 'there's a nice knock-down argument for you!'
>
> But 'glory' doesn't mean 'a nice knock-down argument,' Alice objected.
>
> 'When *I* use a word,' Humpty Dumpty said in rather a scornful tone, 'it means just what I choose it to mean—neither more nor less.'
>
> 'The question is,' said Alice, 'whether you *can* make words mean so many different things.'
>
> 'The question is,' said Humpty Dumpty, 'which is to be master—that's all.[2]

Consider where we are today. Common terms are used by both sides in political debates: the Constitution, rule of law, democracy, etc. But these terms do not mean the same for both. For example, for Republicans and conservatives, the term *rule of law* means an equal standard of justice in which all—regardless of station in life, regardless of the size of one's bank account or one's proximity to power—stand equal before the law, and there is an equal application of the law in all cases. In short, the law is king, much as the Founders intended.

However, for the modern Progressive Statist, the rule of law often means the weaponizing of the law against political opponents. Though that would appear hypocritical on the surface, it isn't to the leftist way of thinking: using the legal system to punish political opponents is their way of implementing and enforcing a hierarchy. For the Left, not all political ideas and beliefs are "created equal." Some are better than others, therefore some should be defended and rewarded and others destroyed because, well, to the Left, those wrong ideas are evil.

Progressive Statists truly believe they are completely justified in using the legal system, the DOJ, and the FBI to enforce their preferred hierarchy because of the rightness of their ways and views. Because they are "right," what they say and do is right and therefore justified. For them the rule of law most certainly does not mean the equal application of the law, but rather its use as a weapon. When a Progressive Statist invokes the Constitution, it is not the Constitution of the Founders with its machinery intact and its separation of powers. With statists, it's the "living" Constitution, the "we can make it do whatever we want it to" Constitution. For example, in the 14th Amendment, passed in the late 1860s to give recently freed slaves full rights as citizens, Progressive Statists see the emanations of penumbras leading to the right to murder unborn children, all in line with Croly's desired "living Constitution" form of "democracy."

To be master of what the Constitution means—that is all.

The statists understand the power of words and the changing of definitions to move the debate in their direction. Grant it, their definitions might have nothing to do with truth, in fact might be the enemy of truth, but they know that if their terms are accepted as they define them, they will win the debate.

Many have heard the quote attributed to Joseph Goebbels: "If you tell a lie big enough and keep repeating it, people will eventually come to believe it." What many have not heard, or are not as familiar with, is the second half of that quote: "The lie can be maintained only for such time as the state can shield the people from the political, economic and/or military consequences of the lie. It thus becomes vitally important for the state to use all of its powers to repress dissent, for the truth is the mortal enemy of the lie, and thus by extension, the truth is the greatest enemy of the state."[3] While there are questions as to whether the quote can be attributed to Goebbels, it does encapsulate why statists despise what they term as "alternative narratives and facts" and why any of those narratives or questions are deemed "misinformation."

Transcendent truth that serves as an objective standard and stands outside of finite time is always the enemy of the state, especially a state that has no desire in advancing the interests of the people. Why? Because truth is a constant reminder of the arbitrary nature of the statist authoritarianism, since truth doesn't change. As Francis Schaeffer pointed out, one of the reasons Christians were killed in the Coliseum in ancient Rome was that, unlike the myriad of religions floating around the Roman Empire at the time, Christianity believed in objective truth, and "no totalitarian authority nor authoritarian state can tolerate those who have an absolute by which to judge that state and its actions."[4] This has always been a problem for authoritarian states: truth can't change. Truth is the truth no matter the time, no matter the place.

But truth is also the enemy of the state because it liberates. The words of Christ still echo down through time: the truth shall set you free—spiritually, but also physically if truly followed. If laws do not align with absolute, natural higher law, those laws are illegitimate. The same is true for terms: if terms and definitions do not line up with transcendent higher law, they are lies.

So consider where we are today in America: is there any real interest in understanding the full truth of so-called Russian collusion? Or understanding the full truth of COVID? Is there interest in having a free and honest press to demand accountability and transparency of the state for it to be more honest?

Of course not. Honesty and truth are not the point on any level.

When it comes to the media, the administrative state is primarily interested in perpetuating the current system via the Approved Narrative. It manages that narrative with the help of corporate propagandists, who attack threats to the state, run interference for state actors, and amplify narratives beneficial to the state. Then, "credentialed experts" are trotted out to "endorse" the Approved Narrative, which the corporate propagandists and state stenographers obediently amplify.

Think about how over the decades a whole host of people have been sent out to bolster certain narratives, being proclaimed as the experts so that the peasants will stop thinking and just listen. Like Third World generals with chests covered in all sorts of medals and ribbons, many of these experts have been "credentialed" by all the right indoctrination centers of higher learning, presenting the false impression that as the experts they have the correct answers, that they are the oracles guiding the dirty and unenlightened masses towards a better future.

But what if all the elite can offer under the guise of facts, data, and science are imperfect, arbitrary ideas? There is no perfect human knowledge set. All they can offer are their thoughts based on presuppositions, biases, and the imperfect practice of science, which is again the pursuit of *greater* knowledge but never the *perfection* of knowledge.

What happens when the interests, beliefs, and opinions of the so-called experts are divergent from the foundational thoughts of this country? For example, what if that belief system of the "expert" class doesn't accept the premise of fallen and imperfect man? What if it has an unwavering belief in the practice of science conducted by imperfect minds via imperfect, biased human beings, and a firm belief that somehow man is perpetually climbing towards perfection—though it is really grasping for the false hope of Babel? But even more so, what if those experts don't really believe in the sanctity of natural, inherent rights? If there is no Higher Being, where does inherent value come from? Or on yet another level, what happens when the belief system of the so-called elites conflicts with that of the majority of the people in the country?

As the French philosopher Jean-Paul Sarte once said, "No finite point has meaning without an infinite reference point."[5] If there is no infinite point of reference, well, then everything becomes arbitrary—or in today's world, whatever the so-called experts say is right. If there are no rights given by a Creator because a Creator doesn't exist, something must give value, even if artificial, to avoid an immediate collapse into the absurd. You have to drive some sort of stake into the ground to anchor society—but then you ultimately end up with government as the giver of rights and value, and the government's experts deciding how value is defined: "if there are no absolutes by which to judge society, then society is absolute."[6]

Once that stage is reached, where society is the absolute and there are no infinite, transcendent absolutes "that provide a final or ultimate standard," then there are no real values, just finite ideas and conflicting opinions.[7] It's a short step from here to simply denying reality, as when suddenly men can be women and women, men—because society at that moment in time says so, and what *is* is right.

Consider the recent example of COVID and Dr. Anthony Fauci, flip-flopping between opposing ideas in short amounts of time. No masks, then masks; the vaccine works and will prevent COVID, then you need several shots and a booster; then, you can still get the virus with masks and more boosters, but it will hopefully mitigate the seriousness of it; then, maybe it wasn't the greatest idea to shoot experimental shots into hundreds of millions of people. To put it mildly, it was a clown show. Fauci was presented as the great expert, but he was more was like the Great and Terrible Wizard of Oz.

In one of the final scenes of *The Wizard of Oz*, Dorothy, the Tin Man, the Cowardly Lion, and the Scarecrow return to the Emerald

City after successfully killing the Wicked Witch of the West, hoping to receive their rewards: a heart, a brain, courage, and for Dorothy, a way home. Upon entering the receiving room of the Great Wizard of Oz, they are in awe of the spectacle: fire and smoke, a massive phantom image, and a thundering voice.

When the companions tell the Wizard that they have succeeded and have come for their rewards, he tells them to come back the next day, but they insist upon staying. He replies, "Do not arouse the wrath and the power of the great Wizard of Oz!" In the midst of their fear and terror, with the Wizard's voice crashing down on them, Toto, Dorothy's little dog, escapes her clutches and runs to a nearby curtain. Pulling it back, Toto reveals a wizened old man, cranking all sorts of levers and speaking into a microphone. The old man, unaware for a few moments that he has been revealed, finally realizes the curtain has been pulled away. He frantically grabs at the curtain, pulling it back as Dorothy and her friends watch in amazement, and then cries out, "Pay no attention to that man behind the curtain!" Dorothy and her friends look on the old man in amazement, sure the Great and Terrible Oz was a terrible beast or a ball of fire. "No, you are all wrong," the old man says, "I have been making believe."[8]

Of course the Wizard of Oz was nothing more than an ordinary man who'd created a land of smoke and mirrors and the myth of the Great Wizard. But when the curtain was pulled back, there was nothing there except an illusion of grandeur, a world of make believe.

It's beginning to feel very much that way with Fauci and the so-called educated elite experts in the 21st century: they're like The Wonderful Wizard of Oz; a mirage, an illusion, an old, wizened man pulling and moving a series of cranks and levers, trying to keep the impression up. But as reality becomes unavoidable, the curtain is being pulled back on the administrative state to show that there is no real *there* there: the so-called experts, while having great power, have no real answers because their entire worldview is arbitrary.

This is the fundamental problem with the intellectual gospel of scientism: the entire Progressive Statist movement—which believes that the application of science via the administrative state, given free rein, would lead to progress—is a house of cards built on a foundation of sand. The absolute belief in imperfect science and trust in imperfect human knowledge can never lead to perfection. It can only lead to the absurd: it is inevitable that if you start with a firm belief and trust in something finite for meaning, all things will eventually devolve into the theater of the absurd.

Take for example eugenics and forced sterilization, bunk race-science embraced by all the leading Progressives of the day, from Wilson and Theodore Roosevelt on down. They worked to implement a state-blessed scientific religion that could regulate marriage, immigration, reproduction all in the name of progress and advancement.

Remember, for Progressive Statists, the state is a living organism. During the 1912 presidential election, Wilson imported the Hegelian idea of "the social organism metaphor to justify his argument for a more powerful and more centralized government." He argued that "Living political constitutions must be Darwinian in structure and practice." Because the social organism "evolved, it should not and probably could not be bound by an unchanging, antiquated set of rules."[9]

So if the state subsumes all as the "living organism," and the goal is efficiency for the living organism, several ideas must follow: there is no individualism, no individual rights to life, liberty, and the pursuit of happiness for all, and no Creator that has endowed life in all forms. There is the state and society, which ultimately deem who and what are necessary for the health of the whole if mankind is to reach the state of apotheosis. And for the whole to be healthy, to progress to a higher plane, anyone or anything deemed parasitical must be ejected. Any imperfection that might slow progress and lead to inefficiency must be dealt with.

Ergo eugenics.

In the early 20th century, for multiple decades, there were many Progressive Statists who were adherents of eugenics. Michael Crichton addresses this issue in a note at the end of his novel *State of Fear* entitled "Why Politicized Science is Dangerous." It's worth quoting at length:

> Imagine that there is a new scientific theory that warns of an impending crisis, and points to a way out. This theory quickly draws support from leading scientists, politicians, and celebrities around the world. Research is funded by distinguished philanthropies, and carried out at prestigious universities. The crisis is reported frequently in the media. The science is taught in college and high school classrooms.
>
> I don't mean global warming. I'm talking about another theory that rose to prominence a century ago.
>
> Its supporters included Theodore Roosevelt, Woodrow Wilson and Winston Churchill. It was approved by Supreme Court Justices Oliver Wendell Holmes and Louis Brandeis, who ruled in its favor.... Research was backed by the Carnegie and Rockefeller Foundations.... Important work was also done at Harvard, Yale, Princeton, Stanford and Johns Hopkins. Legislation to address the crisis was passed in states from New York to California.... Today we know that this famous theory that gained so much support was actually pseudoscience. The crisis it claimed was nonexistent. And the actions taken in the name of this theory were morally and criminally wrong. Ultimately it led to the deaths of millions of people.[10]

The theory Crichton was referring to wasn't global warming or COVID. It was of course eugenics, a pseudoscience that many Progressive Statists were convinced was real science but was actually just scientism, a belief system cloaked in the trappings and verbiage of science and accepted as gospel truth with no empirical evidence to back it up. As Crichton points out, the eugenicists allied with those opposed to immigration and came up with a plan "to identify individuals who are feeble-minded—Jews were agreed to be largely feeble-minded, but so were many foreigners, as well as blacks—and stop them from breeding by isolation in institutions or by sterilization."

These believers in eugenics were the so-called experts, the first believers in scientism and the forerunners to Anthony "I am the Science" Fauci when in fact they were quacks: imagine thinking that blacks or Jews were lesser races because "science." But back then, it was all the rage: science would lead to perfection. *All hail science!* This allowed Progressive Statists to take on the mantle of morality as they discussed forced sterilization of inferior classes, allowed Richard Ely to sneer that "Negroes are for the most part grown up children and should be treated as such,"[11] while others would say, "the black millions of inferior race dragged down American energy and character,"[12] as if the black race retarded progress. Croly, one of the most influential of the Progressive Statists, argued that blacks should not be considered equal to their fellow white citizens and be enfranchised: "The slave holders may have been wrong in enslaving blacks, but they were right in their view that only certain races are capable of self-government...negroes [are] a race possessed of moral and intellectual qualities inferior to those of white men."[13]

John Burgess, the father of political science in America, further wrote, "The claim that there is nothing in the color of skin from the point of political ethics is a great sophism. A black skin means membership in a race of men which has never of itself succeeded...to reason, has never, therefore, created any civilization of any kind." Because of that, it "is the white man's mission, his duty and right, to hold the reins of political power in his own hands."[14] For Progressive Statists, American racial integrity and purity must be protected, so immigrants from certain parts of the world would also be viewed with disdain as Progressives ranted about race suicide. Theodore Roosevelt even announced while still in the White House that "race suicide was the greatest problem of civilization."[15] All of this is deeply ironic in light of the modern-day Progressives' absolute commitment to illegal immigration into the United States; Wilson, Roosevelt, and all the other founding Progressive Statists would be horrified by the sentiment.

All of these eugenicist and racial-purity obsessions would eventually prompt Frank Taussig, a professor of economics at Harvard, to state that the lower classes in society were unemployable and should be simply "stamped out." He wrote: "We've not yet reached the stage where we can proceed to chloroform them once and for all; but at least they can be segregated, shut up in refuges and asylums and prevented from propagating their kind."[16]

One thing leads to the next, and eventually the race-based theory shifted into overt, virulent racism and anti-Semitism. The Progressive pseudoscience of eugenics began losing its appeal in the late 1920s and early '30s in America (but not for the Rockefeller Foundation, which simply moved its research to Germany and was funding German researchers until a few short months before the outbreak of World War II).[17]

To be fair, because of the virulent racism and anti-Semitism of its later advocates, fully applied eugenics became a bridge too far for most American Progressive Statists, despite their hopes of ejecting parasites from the living organism of the state. Most of them, thankfully, couldn't take that belief to its ultimate conclusion. But that didn't prevent German Statism, rising from the same worldview, from taking it all the way to Taussig's envisioned end and "chloroforming" inferior races in Nazi death camps.

As detailed in *Hitler's American Model* by James Q. Whitman, it was in some ways the closing of the circle: the Nazis began looking to American Progressive laws on race, inspired of course by the Prussian Hegel, as the basis for their own laws, which they were determined to take to the ultimate end. In fact, years before the outbreak of World

War II, Nazis began setting up "ordinary-looking houses where mental defects were brought and interviewed one at a time, before being led into a back room, which was, in fact a gas chamber. There, they were gassed with carbon monoxide, and their bodies disposed of in a crematorium located on the property."[18]

When there are no infinite, non-negotiable standards of right and wrong, when you start with an unshakeable faith in the state as all, using the state's imperfect scientism as a veneer of respectability and authority, everything becomes permissible. If it hasn't occurred to you yet, there are powerful elements in American society that view many as parasites to the living organism. You should accept that and then ask yourself what they might do to you if they had the power to do so.

CHAPTER THIRTEEN

WHEN THREATENED, THE STATE STRIKES BACK

The end goal of the Progressives' administrative state is to break down the walls separating the legislative, executive, and judicial powers and fuse them all into one, and as it fuses those powers into one, to separate that power's administration from politics and the accountability that comes with elections. As Ronald J. Pestritto writes, "A government had to be provided to direct and control an industry and governance as a practical matter implied not merely legislative power or simply executive power, but whatever power might be required to achieve the desired results."[1]

The Progressive Statists were never interested in the Constitution as intended, and they weren't shy about it. They stated it clearly, time after time. Consider that the essence of the Constitution is the fundamental protection of natural, inherent rights by the separation and diffusion of power in government. Remove the separation of powers and you gut the Constitution's intent.

What results, gradually and then suddenly, is consolidated power and eventually government thuggery. With massive, consolidated power inside a sprawling bureaucracy, with no checks or balances against that power, removed from accountability to the people's representatives, what comes next is abuse.

The administrative state can't tolerate the idea of limiting its administrators and so-called experts; limitations are anathema to the entire proposition of the state. The Oracles of Progress who reside inside the state, according to the statists, are politically neutral, truly only interested in the welfare and progress of society.

Except that's a lie. There is nothing neutral in life. If anyone tells you that, he or she is lying. Beliefs inform actions, and everyone believes something, even if they won't admit it.

All actions are biased in a certain direction depending on the belief system that informs them. To think otherwise is dangerously naive or intentionally, insidiously evil. Part of the argument made by Wilson, influenced by Hegel, was that somehow those entrusted with massive power to advance society via the state would always be neutral and objective: "Wilson argued that the great task of producing social justice through national governmental programs could be achieved by the use of neutral, 'scientific' administrative methods."[2] This idea of neutrality was an argument and defense of the administrative state, yet to think that somehow the administrative state and its bureaucrats have ever been neutral is absolutely insane, especially in today's America: "It has become clear that the bureaucracy can no longer be understood, or justified in terms of neutrality. The bureaucracy has become a defender of the rational state [administrative state], and it has allied itself with political partisans of both parties in defense of its interest."[3]

For the architects of the administrative state, one key tenet was that administrators be protected from politics and political oversight, because that would be inefficient and somehow taint the process. Besides, they could be trusted, or so the Progressives argued: "The fundamental assumption behind the vast discretion ... given to administrations was a trust or optimism about the selflessness, competence and objectivity of administrators."[4] Wilson, Croly, and the other early Progressives knew they were playing with fire and that the administrative state would weaken the protection of individual rights. And they went ahead and built it anyway.

But what happens when a certain, and not insignificant, percentage of society questions whether the administrative state is actually working for society's best interests? What happens when it begins to resist the Oracles of the state? Such behavior is considered dangerous, undermining, to the state, and so it mobilizes against them.

Consider Richard Nixon and the leftist fantasy of Watergate, and understand what it was really all about. During his re-election campaign for a second term in the White House, Nixon made it abundantly clear that he was intent on restoring constitutionalism and representative government to the United States. He refused to accept the administrative state as legitimate, and his attacks "on the governmental bureaucracy constituted an implicit repudiation of the Progressive view legitimized by the New Deal, and made operative in the Great Society.... the purpose of his policy of decentralization and executive reorganization...was to restore a representative government."[5] His ideas were well received: in the 1972 presidential elections, Nixon received 520 electoral votes, won 49 states, and got over 60 percent of the popular vote, crushing George McGovern by nearly 20 million votes.

And then came Watergate.

Nixon had made it very clear what he intended to do to the administrative state if he was re-elected, and in 1972, after one of the more definitive re-elections in American history, he absolutely "posed the greatest danger to the authority of the bureaucracy and the administrative state."[6] There is no need to delve into the history of Watergate and the war that took place between the duly elected president and the bureaucracy, buttressed by its allies in the corporate press and Congress. But it is interesting to note how eerily similar Richard Nixon's situation was to Donald Trump's: the "legendary" Deep Throat of Bob

Woodward and Carl Bernstein was a high-level FBI official, Mark Felt, who leaked classified information to Woodward and Bernstein, really turning the two supposed "investigative reporters" into "conduits by which the bureaucracy could undermine the authority of an elected officeholder."[7] So in short, a high-level FBI official worked with the corporate propagandists to bring down the duly elected president of the United States. Some might call that behavior treason.

Which means Watergate and Russiagate are in many ways two sides of the same coin. The war between the administrative state and those who are a threat to it, either by explicitly targeting it or by simply resisting and dissenting with it, continues to this day. Consider Donald J. Trump. Consider the parents protesting at school board meetings who were targeted by the DOJ and considered by some on the Left as domestic terrorists.

As the administrative state is seeking to delegitimize duly elected leaders like Donald Trump and ordinary citizens like concerned parents, it is also imposing its skewed social and political agenda on society to achieve policy ends it cannot achieve through elections or Congress. Consider Operation Chokepoint at the Departments for Justice, Treasury, and Commerce, in which the administrative state pressures banks and other financial institutions to deny loans and capital to industries the state doesn't approve of, such as manufacturers of ammunition and gun dealers. Or the Securities and Exchange Commission's climate-change and Environmental, Social, and Corporate Governance (ESG) shareholder rules, or the FCC's Net Neutrality regulations, or the Consumer Financial Protection Bureau, which receives funding without Congressional oversight or review, and with its absurd and opaque standards may decide, by fiat, what are abusive practices or not, including even companies making a profit being abusive if it so determines.

None of the above initiatives was proposed by Congress, nor necessarily supported or implemented by a White House. Yet all are a reality because the administrators are the ones governing, they are the ones deciding, and they are hell-bent on making this country a creature of their own via their sub-delegated and extra-legislative methods. There are many other examples of this throughout the government, but the point is that the unelected bureaucrats are governing, and if you really and truly question them and the status quo of their state, you're considered a threat—and threats cannot be tolerated, however small.

It's becoming more and more apparent that the DOJ and FBI are nothing less than the administrative state's Praetorian Guard, the ruling class's personal bodyguards, intelligence gatherers, and intimidators. They aren't protecting the rights of the American people and haven't done so for decades. But they are hell-bent on attacking their political enemies, protesting parents, and anyone who dares question the state and whether justice is truly taking place. As Marini writes, "The bureaucracy has itself become a political faction on behalf of administrative rule .... the defenders of administrative government are increasingly unable to understand, let alone tolerate, those who fail to recognize or accept the legitimacy of the administrative state."[8]

Think about it: if you do not submit to what the ruling class of the administrative state wants, whether you're Donald Trump or a concerned parent, these supposed guardians of the rule of law will try to frame you with false conspiracy theories or show up at school board meetings, menacing people into silence. They will break down your door like they did to James O'Keefe and seize evidence harmful to their cause or allies (in most cases, the Democrat Party). Then they will spill the beans to a Left-wing propagandist outlet, of which there are so many to choose.

If you refuse to be obedient serfs in the feudal administrative state, you will feel the force and wrath of the state.

What should concern all Americans, regardless of political persuasion, is that there are no limits to the Justice Department and FBI's abuse. They spent four years searching for dirt on the sitting president of the United States, only for their so-called evidence to be revealed as a hoax.

They needed only the slimmest excuse to abuse the FISA process and attack a political enemy whom they viewed as an existential threat, and they used that slimmest of excuses (the Steele Dossier) not once but four times. So it shouldn't come as a surprise that if they're willing to target the duly elected president of the United States, they're more than willing to target innocent everyday citizens.

That is why the FBI and Justice Department should cease to exist in their current forms, if they should even exist at all. The next Republican president needs to make it very clear that he will put reform-minded people in positions of power at the FBI, the Justice Department, and, quite frankly, throughout the bureaucracy. The administrative state must be broken up in all its current corrupt forms. And once these are broken up, the remains need to be displayed for all to see how deep the corruption truly runs. When the next Republican wins the White House, one of his first executive orders, hopefully made in tandem with Congressional leadership, should announce the formation of a new Church Committee with public hearings and televised testimony to show the American public how deep the abuse has been with the DOJ, the FBI, and the surveillance state. Only then can we rebuild those parts of the government into something that is much smaller and focused on doing what it is supposed to do—upholding the rule of law as a fundamental principle of our society while actually serving the people.

This mindset should be applied to every department and agency inside the administrative state. Every aspect of the state is politicized and is committed to a certain political worldview. That is why some of us were deeply skeptical of the NIH and CDC at the very beginning of COVID, especially after witnessing the highly political DOJ and FBI. Some wrongly assumed the NIH and CDC were pure as driven snow, seeking only what's best for the American people. Others, correctly, viewed them as different branches of the same poisonous tree of the administrative state and were highly skeptical of Fauci, the vaccine, the models showing apocalyptic death tolls—in short, almost everything. In the future, any time anyone from the government makes an outlandish claim, the first response and question should be, "Is it actually true?" And the next question must be, "Can you really prove it?"

CHAPTER FOURTEEN

THE ULTIMATE END OF PROGRESSIVISM IS AUTHORITARIANISM

The entire premise of the administrative state has been proven a farce. The goal for Wilson and other Progressive Statists in the early 20th century was to give incredible power to "the best boys from the best colleges" with as little political oversight as possible, all supposedly to advance society with applied science. Which is precisely how you end up with Fauci, Comey, Brennan, Clapper, and every other out-of-control bureaucrat who thinks he knows what's absolutely best. This is the opposite of progress and a regression into authoritarianism via the empowerment of petty, abusing tyrants spread across the vast bureaucracy.

After a century of experiment, the administrative state's power is concentrated in the hands of a credentialed idiocracy who believe they are the final arbiters for government and society, working to perpetuate the status quo for the good of themselves and their allies, not the American people.

As with every other form of statism throughout the entire history of the world, the ultimate end of Progressivism is inevitably authoritarianism. In fact, that is exactly the point of Hegel's writings from two hundred years ago. For him, as Popper describes it, history progressed this way: "The first of these steps is Oriental despotism, the second is formed by the Greek and Roman democracies and aristocracies, and the third, the highest, is the Germanic Monarchy, which of course is an absolute monarchy."[1]

The inspiration for the American Progressive Statists, the man whose ideas they embraced and implemented, believed that the authoritarianism of an absolute monarchy was in fact the pinnacle and "end of history." For perspective, Hegel was writing these things and lecturing on them decades after the founding of the free American Republic, which apparently wasn't the pinnacle of history in his eyes.

If you draw your inspiration from Hegel and his beliefs and glorification of authoritarianism, you can only end up in one place. If you believe and advocate in the administrative state, have bought into the massive, sprawling bureaucracy filled with an "educated elite," and believe it is the vehicle for progress to a glorious future, then debate, dissent, and resistance to the state are in fact resistance to progress. If you believe that you have placed in motion the "march of God on earth" towards utopia with your educated elite and all-powerful bureaucracy, then all who question it are apostates, backwards, deplorables, the irredeemables, dirty little peasants.

Which means they are threats in the eyes of the state, and can be destroyed.

This administrative-state mindset is what leads many to believe representative democracy is tired and backwards. God forbid that the backwards peasants should actually be allowed to vote in free and fair elections and potentially derail progress! Progressive Statists are not interested in representative democracy in the least. They are in fact opposed to it: they have zero interest in truly free and fair elections, where the people's representatives actually go on to govern. If those elected could actually exercise the power delegated to them by the

Constitution, well, the American people might return believing that elections have consequences. That would bring about a power shift, accountability, and transparency—which Progressive Statists cannot allow to happen. But even more so, they can't allow the terrifying idea that we might return to the Dark Ages when covenants and the protection of free and just associations, along with separation of powers and accountability, are restored.

With its absolute faith in the progress of scientism and the so-called educated elite, the philosophy of the administrative state is a secular religion, with sacraments, creeds, priests, and all the other trappings of a belief system: rights come from the government as it deems fit; society is directed by the elites, who are the oracles of the state; the state is right; you are wrong. President Eisenhower saw some of this coming and noted it in his famous farewell address to the nation in 1961. After highlighting the dangers of the military-industrial complex, Eisenhower said,

> Akin to, and largely responsible for the sweeping changes in our industrial-military posture, has been the technological revolution during recent decades. In this revolution, research has become central; it also becomes more formalized, complex, and costly. A steadily increasing share is conducted for, by, or at the direction of, the Federal government.... The prospect of domination of the nation's scholars by Federal employment, project allocations, and the power of money is ever present— and is gravely to be regarded. Yet, in holding scientific research and discovery in respect, as we should, we must also be alert to the equal and opposite danger *that public policy could itself become the captive of a scientific-technological elite* [emphasis added].[2]

Eisenhower warned of our present situation. Of course, the present situation has been the entire goal of Progressive Statism all along: the

Oracles of Scientism and the "educated elite" proclaim what is good and right progress for society, the propagandists in the media reinforce that, and the indoctrination centers of higher learning reinforce that. Those who question and prevent progress must be ostracized and dealt with harshly for their unbelief.

This is because Progressive Statism is a secular religion based on scientism.

And because of their absolute faith in scientism, Progressive Statists are fundamentalists in their beliefs. That means there is no debate: they are right, and those who disagree are wrong. Why would one debate someone who is rejecting the pure gospel of scientism? Why would you debate someone who is so backwards and blinded as to fight progress, the march of history to the apotheosis of man? You don't debate; you demand submission. The apostates must either convert or be destroyed. The entire attitude and approach of Progressives smacks of the rise of Islam and conversion by the sword, which is where we are headed today if we aren't careful: convert and accept Progressive Statism and its administrative state, or you will be forced to comply. You can be sure Progressives would be far more aggressive if it weren't for the 2nd Amendment and a hundred million armed Americans. That's one of the greatest bulwarks against the state's advances, and the statists know it.

Always understand that when you confront such religious zealotry, you must expect retaliatory harshness in return. Ask yourself what will happen, if left unchecked, when the state finally has had enough, and even more so, bolstered by propagandists and an "intelligentsia," feels justified in forcibly moving against dissenters? It begins slowly: perhaps the aspects of government that used to be the guardians of the rule of law are now weaponized against political opponents. Submit and comply or else. Questions about the legitimacy and fairness of elections are *verboten*, especially if the elections are favorable to Progressive Statists. Show trials are put in place to ostracize political dissenters and forestall said questions.

All of that, however, is just the end of the beginning.

It could get far worse if history is to be our guide. There are always steps towards the edge of the abyss before the cataclysmic plunge off the cliff. The outcasts who question must be dehumanized, and when dehumanized they are less than qualified to be a part of "proper society." As with all statists throughout time, those who resist them or are deemed a threat by them must be dehumanized; it's the *untermeschen* strategy of the demented little German man with the funny mustache, who in the 1930s raged non-stop against a certain segment of society and, once he'd gained power and persuaded enough of the German people he was right, could do to that segment of society whatever he wanted to. And he did. If one can succeed in dehumanizing, or sub-humanizing, a segment of society, making them enemies of the state and society, then one can do with sub-humans whatever one wants to do.

CHAPTER FIFTEEN

LEVIATHAN TODAY

So where are we today, just over a century after the Progressive Statist experiment became reality in America? What began as small and mostly theoretical, but with the premise of becoming central to the American way of life, has in fact turned into the massive, sprawling Leviathan of the administrative state that the early Progressive Statists dreamed of. Like the reinforcing loops discussed earlier, the administrative state began slowly in the beginning of the 20th century with Wilson, but the premise and legitimacy were gradually accepted. Then, with multiple waves of Progressive Statist expansion, and the abdication of Congress, it grew and grew, until suddenly, like compounding interest, it has absolutely exploded in size the last several decades.

It's hard to fully comprehend its breadth at the federal level; in fact there is no agreement on its actual size. There are somewhere over 430 departments, agencies, sub-agencies, and commissions inside the federal government today; some sources list 440, and others 443.[1] Those include of course the major departments such as state, Defense, Treasury, Labor, Interior, and the rest. But there are also entities like the Bureau of Reclamation, the Bureau of Safety and Environmental Enforcement, and the Centers for Medicare and Medicaid Services, because of course every time a new federal government program is begun, a corresponding office or agency must be spun up to manage the program, which includes, again of course, more spending to manage the spending.

Inside and associated with this bureaucracy are "Nearly 9.1 million workers, comprising nearly 6 percent of total employment in the United States. The figure includes nearly 2.1 million federal employees, 4.1 million contract employees, 1.2 million grant employees, 1.3 million active duty military personnel, and more than 500,000 postal service employees."[2] And that figure from four years ago is likely low as government continues to grow, with the total in 2024 in all probability closer to 10 million workers for the Leviathan. If one adds state and local government employees, of which there are over 20 million, then you have roughly 30 million government workers in America. That would mean that close to 20 percent of the entire workforce is working, either directly or by contract, for the government.

Those federal workers are well compensated, too: the average salary for a government employee at the federal level is over $90,000 a year. But of the over two million federal employees, more than a third are GS-12 or higher, meaning that in the middle and upper echelons of the administrative state, there are hundreds of thousands of government employees making six-figure salaries.

The premise was that these federal government employees, the "educated elite," the "best boys from the best colleges," would be highly educated to help lead society to a bright and glorious future. However, according to statistics, almost 75 percent of them have only a bachelor's degree or lower—which tells us that the entire idea of them having a highly educated elite to guide society has been abandoned.[3]

The annual federal budget for this is monstrosity was $6.1 trillion in 2022, or about 25 percent of our entire GDP. And it's not as though it's being well spent. Take for example the Department of Defense, which admits it can't account for $2.2 trillion of its supposed assets: only "39 percent of the [DoD's] $3.5 trillion in assets are accounted for."[4] Over the course of decades, hundreds of billions of dollars have simply disappeared inside the Pentagon: the Department of Defense has been unable to pass a single independent financial audit since its first one in 2017, and of the twenty-seven agencies audited within the Department of Defense, only seven received a passing grade. Realize that the money and assets missing inside our Department of Defense alone is higher than the annual GDP of Canada, Russia, or Italy, all of which are among the top ten economies in the world.

And that waste is just with Defense.

When one keeps peeling back the onion, you realize the lumbering, lurching, slovenly beast of Leviathan loses and wastes incredible amounts of money every single day just through its inefficiencies: taxpayer money is wasted on renaming schools, roads, and bridges rather than rebuilding the crumbling infrastructure already in place; Secretary of Transportation Pete Buttigieg plans to spend $1 billion on "racial equity" in roads.[5] Right now, we have over 770,000 empty federal buildings that the government owns and maintains, costing taxpayers more than $1.7 billion a year.[6] We still have no real idea about what's really happened to the $200 billion going to Ukraine: none of the agencies we're funding keep tabs on whose hands it goes into once it's there. Because of the money flowing during the COVID "pandemic," $286 million in COVID relief funds were fraudulently granted and then eventually re-seized by the US Secret Service. As of 2023, Medicare and Medicaid fraud is now reckoned at $100 billion annually, though the real figure might be higher.[7] And there's the $11.6 million that the IRS spent to purchase unused software. The list could go on and on, but the picture is pretty clear: the inept, wasteful administrative state that was supposed to be the efficient vehicle to progress is anything but efficient.

Back when the Progressive Statists advocated for and implemented the administrative state, one of their arguments was that more bureaucracy meant a healthier, more efficient, and more advanced society. It was a lie back then, but it is even more of a lie today: the ugly Leviathan of government is an emblem of decline, a teetering monstrosity that barely works, all built on the incredibly naïve idea that man can be perfected in an imperfect world. Yet we as a country continue to stagger forward with this massive beast on our backs, and with every passing year, the beast weighs heavier and heavier. At some point in the not-so-distant future, unless the trajectory changes, it will completely crush the American people.

The litany of government wastes could go for pages on end and would still just be scratching the surface. Now juxtapose that mind-boggling excess with the Internal Revenue Service's goal of nearly 100 percent growth from its current 93,600 employees with the hiring of 87,000 new employees, nearly 50,000 of whom would be agents with the capacity and expectation of using deadly force on citizens in the completion of their responsibilities.[8]

Let that sink in: the IRS wants to have over 180,000 employees with tens of thousands of new agents who are essentially armed revenue agents meant to soak the middle class. If you think that sounds like the British revenue agents in pre-Revolutionary America, you wouldn't be wrong. But for perspective on the potentially new IRS, the Department of Justice has roughly 115,000 employees over 40 departments; the new and more powerful IRS would dwarf that. Moreover, the new agents would be there not to go after the billionaires and millionaires but to hoover up taxes on $600 PayPal transactions. Even if one were to put 90 percent tax rates on the wealthy, there are only so many of them. Better by far, in Progressive Statist thinking, to increase the taxes of the potentially hundreds of millions, because that's the only way to substantially increase real funding for Leviathan. This was always the point with the income tax and the IRS: redistribution of wealth and the funding of the administrative state.

Add that to the increasing arrogance of the federal government, which was originally meant to serve the American people: instead of cutting the waste and potentially finding hundreds of billions of dollars a year, the solution for the voracious administrative state is to soak up more money from the people, by force. This is also how you get inflation: more government, more government spending, more money in circulation. Not only are you taxed more to feed the beast, the money you have left is now worth less.

Speaking of force, consider the DOJ, FBI, IRS and DoD: these are all already massive departments and agencies. They are also extremely powerful, with the ability to destroy individual lives through the overwhelming force of the government, to grind you into submission or show up on your doorstep heavily armed, to crush under their thumbs anyone who might actually question the administrative state. No one is immune from their abuse of power; Donald J. Trump, as sitting president of the United States, found that out the hard way.

Not only is the administrative state fundamentally unconstitutional, but the leadership of many of the government agencies also treat any perceived oversight with extreme dismissiveness. Take for example Christopher Wray of the FBI. He essentially cut short a Senate oversight hearing because he claimed he had important business elsewhere, which turned out to be flying on the FBI's jet to his vacation home.[9] Or even more egregious, James Clapper's lying under oath to the Senate that he didn't spy on American citizens when in fact he did.[10] Not only did Clapper continue on as the head of DNI, there were absolutely zero consequences for his perjury. Today, Clapper remains one of the voices who has pushed the Russian collusion hoax and the idea that Hunter Biden's laptop was Russian disinformation, again, with zero consequences.

It's not that anyone didn't see this coming. Back in December 1963, a decade after his presidency, Harry Truman began to have serious concerns with the CIA. The agency began during Truman's first administration with the intent of it being the "quiet intelligence arm of the President." But it quickly became something that Truman described as being far beyond what he'd imagined: "For some time I have been

disturbed by the way CIA has been diverted from its original assign-
ment. It has become an operational and at times a policy-making arm
of the Government. This has led to trouble and may have compounded
our difficulties in several explosive areas."[11]

Consider how quickly the CIA went off the rails in Truman's estimation. It was in 1947 that he signed the National Security Act, which
established the agency. Within sixteen years it had morphed into
something that so deeply troubled him, a "policy-making arm of the
Government," that he felt compelled to write a public opinion piece
about it in one of the leading newspapers of the day.

Yet what Truman apparently missed is that the CIA's transformation into a policymaking arm is pretty much exactly the point of the
administrative state: powerful unelected bureaucrats become the poli-
cymakers in this country. But let Truman's warning from 1963 sink in:
if he was concerned about the CIA sixty years ago, what has it become
today? Well, for starters, we've ended up with the head of the CIA,
John Brennan, helping amplify and drive the Russian-collision narrative against the duly elected president of the United States. Egregious
as that is, it's not a shock and hardly the worst thing the CIA has done
in the last several generations.

Over the course of time, the American people have fallen asleep in
the light. Most have grown used to the vastness of the administrative
state and numb to its increasingly painful prescriptions, which are meant
to cow the sovereign American people into servitude: ever-increasing
taxes and fees heaped on half the citizenry, while the other half pay
nothing; ever-more-intimidating federal law enforcement (including the
IRS), who see a binary world in which they are the good guys and the rest
of guilty crooks who just haven't been caught yet (think early-morning
raids on a Catholic father of seven by twenty-five armed FBI agents,
who was acquitted by a jury in less than an hour); a "Justice" Department that no longer has standards for investigation and prosecution
but uses process as punishment—as if throwing darts at the dartboard

to see what charges could be brought against innocent businessmen, who when faced with the crushing expense of defending themselves for years on end, often plead out just to make the misery stop.

And while this is going on in front of our eyes, most of the country, thinking it has nothing to do with them, just yawns and goes back to watching reality TV.

At some point, this type of arrogant, thuggish behavior from unelected administrative-state actors, if left unchecked, will continue to get worse—as is always the case in life when there are no consequences. No one from the FBI or DOJ went to jail for their abuse of the FISA process to secure four warrants off a bogus Steele Dossier to target the duly elected president of the United States. As there were zero consequences for that, there is no deterrent for even worse behavior in the future. It stands to reason we can expect even worse behavior from administrative-state actors in the future until there are severe enough consequences to make sure it never happens again.

CHAPTER SIXTEEN

SLAY LEVIATHAN: BREAK THE STATE, DRAIN THE SWAMP, RESTORE THE REPUBLIC

The barbarians aren't just at the gates in this country. They're inside the gates. Even more so, they are in positions of power across government and most of society.

The un-American Progressive Statists who embrace authoritarianism, destroy property rights, annihilate individual rights, crush political and civil liberties, free expression, the free flow of information, the freedom of movement if they could—who want to invade every aspect of your life and mold you into their vision for society as they demand submission—are in control of almost every major institution in America.

They wield immense power and are intent on doing all of the above in pursuit of their misguided view of progress via the Great and Glorious administrative state. They have in effect declared war on a hundred fronts against the Founders' Republic and the American people's way of life, yet they blame the American people and call those who actually attempt to represent the people's interests divisive and disruptive when they resist Progressive Statism. And when the American people and their representatives resist, they are accused of being backwards, irredeemable deplorables, simply for wanting to restore the Republic.

To state the obvious: it is not the American people who have created the divisiveness.

Most would prefer to be left alone to live in peace, raise their families, worship God, and pursue their talents. And yet the pernicious Progressives insist on their war against the Founders, against the original intent of the Constitution, until all submit to their belief system. We would have peaceful lives, but they would have political war to reshape this country into their warped vision, so it is most assuredly the Progressive Statists who are the divisive ones. We must be clear on this: the pushback against statism and hope for the restoration of rights and the Republic by the American people and Donald Trump is exactly what the un-American Left views as disruptive. To which we must respond: "We will give you all the disruption you want."

There is no other way to put it: it is time to declare political war on the administrative state, to tear it apart piece by piece, and to restore the Republic.

It's obvious that the modern-day Democratic Party is not the party of JFK, or even Bill Clinton for that matter. It is a radical, leftist party that fully embraces realizing its un-American statist roots. Its god is the state, its religion politics and power, its creed an intellectually incoherent mess of global warming, transgenderism, globalism, and infanticide. Its adherents hate this country and they hate you. You cannot reason with people with which you have zero grounds for agreement. Because of that, to return to normal, the Progressive Statists and the un-American Left must be beaten into political submission until they sue for terms—which will be unconditional surrender. There is no other path to sanity except that one. If anyone thinks otherwise, they are deeply naive: oil and water will never mix.

And then we must return as a nation to a set of common ideals and understanding, beginning with the belief there will never, ever be heaven on earth, no Kingdom of God in the here and now, no apotheosis of man. Hegel and his statism must be rejected and we must embrace the Founders again, especially their optimistic realism on the nature of man. We must accept, as the great Thomas Sowell once said in an interview with Fred Barnes, that "Man is flawed from day one. There are no solutions, only trade-offs."[1] Will we see glimpses of heaven? Of course. Will there be goodness? Yes, in some form. Will there be justice? Yes, in some form. Will we see glimpses of perfection? Of course. But in an imperfect world filled with imperfect people, total perfection this side of eternity, in any aspect of life, will never be achieved. We must abandon this fool's errand.

We as human beings are capable of great good, but incapable of sustained good. There is nothing wrong in acknowledging that. What is wrong, however, is to defy that reality, because to do so is naively to believe that consolidated power can be placed in the hands of imperfect people who many times do what they can, not what they should. It is defiance of the reality of human nature that put us on this dangerous path as a country. It must be rejected.

We must return to the belief in imperfect human nature and the implementation of the separation of powers in reality: the administrative state, with its consolidated power and separation of administration from political accountability, and the constitutional republic, built on the entire premise of the separation and diffusion of powers and accountability to the people, cannot exist together. The administrative state is the antithesis of the Republic and must be rejected wholesale.

Back in the days of the Roman Republic, Cato the Elder understood the threat Carthage presented to Rome. Although Rome had managed to defeat Carthage in the two previous Punic Wars, the North African nation was rising again. After visiting Carthage in person, Cato returned home to Rome, convinced that if the Republic did not immediately address the rising threat to the south, it might not go so well for Rome in a potential third war with Carthage. From that moment on, during every speech he gave on the Senate floor, regardless of the topic, Cato would end his speech with *Carthago delenda est*—"Carthage must be destroyed"—because it was an existential threat to the future of the Roman Republic. And finally, in the end, Cato had his way: several years after he began his campaign against Carthage on the floor of the Roman Senate, the Third Punic War began. The war was fought entirely on Carthaginian soil, and in his final victory over the Carthaginians, the Roman commander, Scipio, broke down Carthage's city walls and, according to legend, sowed its fields with salt. Carthage lay in ruins for a century.

In much the same vein, the next Republican president must declare war on the administrative state on day one of his administration and then by all means necessary devolve and destroy it: *gubernatio administrativa delenda est*. His White House must be staffed with people who believe that the state must be dismantled wholesale—not managed, not trimmed around the edges, but taken apart piece by piece, with whatever remains being directly responsive to the president. This is why the next Republican president must get the Office of Presidential Personnel right from the very beginning.

In every administration there is something called the Plum Book, which lists out roughly five thousand political-appointee positions that a president can place throughout the various departments and agencies inside the executive branch. These positions range from low-level Schedule C appointments (1,300 or so) to of course the secretaries, assistant secretaries, and other higher-level decision-making positions. Every last one of those positions, especially the ones with real decision-making authority (hundreds, but less than a thousand), must be done right. Those appointees must be on the same page and understand that they are being sent into the various departments and agencies with the goal of breaking the administrative state. When the bureaucrats stall, hide behind emails, and kill proposals by slow-walking them, those appointees must be willing to fight, determined every day to break the state.

That intentional bureaucratic stalling is of course a perversion of the Founders' vision for the role of the executive. They believed that the president of the United States was fully in charge of the executive branch and that upon being sworn in to office, he should be able to implement his vision for domestic and foreign policy. Any checks and balances on the executive inside the federal government were to come from the other two branches, the judicial and legislative.

But what Progressive Statists inside the executive branch have decided is that when a Republican president is in the White House, they will unconstitutionally check his power by slow-walking, stalling, and killing proposals simply because they don't agree with them. They in fact justify that behavior openly, claiming the Founders wanted bureaucrats inside the executive branch to check the executive. That is simply untrue: any and all who reside in the executive branch are to work for and advance the policies of the chief executive, not act as some check on the executive's power.

Recently, the president of the National Treasury Employees Union, which represents federal employees in thirty-four different federal agencies and departments, ranted about how the federal employees were neutral and don't play politics with their jobs and that a president has no right to attack the nearly two million federal employees who might be stymieing the his agenda: "Federal employees right now swear an oath to uphold the Constitution, but these proposals (from Trump) are more like swearing an oath to a politician, and it is autocratic.... I'm no historian, but the debate over whether the US would have an executive with unchecked power was settled nearly 250 years ago."[2] That's simply a lie used to justify the unconstitutional behavior of the Progressive Statist bureaucrats.

Congress must decide that it will truly govern again, that it will legislate and make the real laws: "Congress ... should bar judicial deference to agencies on questions of law or fact, as this violates due process and other constitutional limitations.... Congress should remove immunity for administrators—beginning with those who have desk jobs at agencies with a track record of violating constitutional rights."[3] As that process unfolds, there should also be a legislative process instituted by which all regulations are examined and passed, or rejected, by Congress. For example, a regulation must be publicly posted for ninety days so Congress can read, discuss, and debate it before it comes to a vote. That's how a democratic republic should work, not by legislation via bureaucratic fiat.

But as it can be assumed that Congress is feckless and filled with gutless wonders and swamp creatures, a Republican in the White House should set in motion a process to devolve the state. There are ways to do it with powers already vested in the executive branch, where, again, most of the administrative state resides. The first can be **Mass Firings or Reduction in Force Exercises**. Each agency has the authority to abolish positions it deems unnecessary. These are called "Reduction in Force" (RIF) exercises, and an agency can do it for a variety of reasons. One is simply reorganizing the agency to become more efficient. The president could direct all his cabinet secretaries to engage in a reorganization of their agencies and have them identify which positions should be abolished and which are essential. The president can then legally abolish thousands of government positions in each agency, and the people filling those positions would be fired.

Of the nearly two million federal civilian employees, there are 800,000 non-essential federal employees on the rolls. You could call that the "DMV state" (DC, Maryland, Virginia area), which is mostly an incompetent, moronic bureaucracy of hundreds of thousands filling the ugly, slovenly Leviathan who basically do nothing—different from the very powerful and problematic surveillance or deep state. Some refer to the DMV state as "retired in place" because of the infinitesimal amount of work its employees do. There's not much accountability, and it is hard to fire them even though they really just exist to collect a paycheck. Hire friends and family to live off the American taxpayer, those lazy bureaucrats have an "iron rice bowl" and vote to perpetuate the system that drains the lifeblood out of the American people.

It's time to end the statists' patronage system where the American taxpayer foots the bill. For so many different reasons a Republican president with any iota of self-preservation would end it, including but not limited to, the ending of laundering of taxpayer dollars into political contributions for Democrats.[4] There is no reason that the federal departments and agencies should not be cut by 40 percent, at a minimum, over the first four years of an America First Republican president. It's much like when Elon Musk first acquired Twitter (now X) and fired nearly 90 percent of the staff. There was great outcry by some, but within weeks it became apparent that Twitter was working just fine, maybe even better. It would be the same with our government losing those 800,000 non-essential employees: it can be almost guaranteed the American people would never notice as their lives would be no worse, but likely better.

If a Republican president wanted to take a gentler approach to reducing the federal workforce, there are tools for that. Bureaucrats can be bought out using **Voluntary Separation Incentive Payments** (one could pay them whatever amount one sees fit), and they can be offered early retirement using the **Voluntary Early Retirement Authority**. Another tool for mass reductions in the administrative state would be **Reassignment**: you can reassign bureaucrats in Washington, DC, to a remote location, and if they refuse to accept the transfer, you are then allowed to fire them. The Director of the Office of Personnel Management has the authority to manage this and could assist cabinet secretaries in using all of the above tools to effectively gut each federal agency down to its bare essentials.

Another tool for a president would be **Presidential In-Person Agency Visits**. Whenever the president tells one of his cabinet secretaries to enact a conservative policy, there's a high likelihood it will get intentionally stalled at some point in the bureaucratic process.

A solution to this is having the president of the United States physically visit the agency and tell bureaucrats to their face to carry out his orders. If they refuse, they are insubordinate to their chief constitutional officer and can be fired on the spot for cause by the president. If they sue, that's perfectly fine—it would be to our benefit for a case of a president directly firing an insubordinate civil servant to reach the now-conservative Supreme Court.

One way this specific process could work would be to have the president issue orders to his cabinet secretary and periodically visit the agency to check on the progress. The president would come equipped with his team, which includes his White House counsel. When the cabinet secretary gives the president an excuse for why something hasn't gotten done, the president and his team will solve it right there by either firing the bureaucrat who is slowing it down or getting the bureaucrat to comply. This may seem extreme, but there is precedent for it: Vice President Dick Cheney did a version of this setting up a personal office to work out of in all the most important federal agencies. And in reality, a president would probably only have to do it once or twice before word traveled around and the remaining bureaucrats at every federal agency fell in line.

Another tool for a president to devolve the administrative state would be to **Wage War on the Bureaucrats through the Office of Personnel Management (OPM)**. OPM has broad discretion to set the pay, health insurance, retirement benefits, and promotion requirements for federal employees. With the right director of OPM in place, a president could use that control to beat the bureaucrats into submission. To further highlight the importance of it all, the OPM director should be brought into the president's cabinet. His or her job would basically be to rein in the deep state; OPM has the tools to do that, one of which could be to **Convert "Career Reserved" Senior Executive Service (SES) Positions to "General" Using OPM**. "Career-reserved" is basically Schedule F but for the Senior Executive Service (SES), which is the senior-most level of bureaucrat (just below Senate-confirmed appointees). Many of these SES positions are reserved so that only a career bureaucrat can serve in them. But OPM can reclassify them so that a political appointee of the president can serve there instead. Doing this would allow a deeper level of political control over the nuts and bolts of each federal agency.

Another step would be to **Gut the Office of Management and Budget (OMB) by Getting Rid of the President's Budget.** The OMB is essentially the citadel of the administrative state, with 90 percent of the staff being career bureaucrats who have the power to distribute hundreds of millions, if not billions, of discretionary spending, which they typically direct to leftist groups. It is the clearinghouse of regulations, truly the epicenter of government by fiat of unelected bureaucrats. One of the supposed reasons for the OMB's existence is the president's budget, which has become a futile exercise where the OMB spends months laboring over every federal dollar spent and then submits a budget to Congress that then gets completely ignored. Instead of wasting all this time, the president should use OMB to determine a few big asks they have of Congress and simply submit those only, saying they won't sign a budget unless those requests are met.

For example, instead of submitting an entire federal budget, which gave the Left ammunition to attack him for proposed cuts to programs, President Trump could have just said he needed funding for his wall on the southern border and identified a couple of programs where it could've been allocated. This gives more weight to the president's request because he's not asking Congress to change the budget of a million different programs that don't matter. It also guts the OMB bureaucracy maybe by half; without the president's budget, they'll have no reason to exist and their positions can be abolished. Then, whichever OMB career staff are left should then be removed from the Eisenhower Building and placed in the New Executive Office Building across the street or back in Treasury—no need for powerful administrative state bureaucrats walking the halls of the offices where most of the Republican president's political appointees are housed. This also frees up politically appointed OMB staff to deal with the important work of minimizing waste, fraud, and abuse in government grants.

As we saw with the Ukrainian quid-pro-quo farce, the National Security Council (NSC) must be reformed, so the president must **Bring NSC Personnel under the Control of the White House Presidential Personnel Office**. Right now, the hiring of the bureaucrats who make up the NSC is not under the authority of the White House. It has its own HR department, allowing career employees to hire each other—which is insane. That's how people like Lt. Col. Alexander "Chow Thief" Vindman got in. The right NSC director can change that and effectively make the positions political appointments.

The president can also **Reinstate Civil-Service Exams**. Civil-service exams still exist for foreign-service officers, the postal service, and air traffic controllers. But for the vast majority of government employees, they were eliminated years ago. They should be brought back to make the workforce of better quality and more patriotic. Prospective government employees should be asked questions about American history, the original intent of the Constitution and our Republic, and our culture. The OPM director has broad authority to mandate these tests and create whatever questions they want to ask, making this is another useful tool for devolving the state.

Another could be the **Schedule F Approach**. The Schedule F process basically makes the lower-level policymaking bureaucrats between GS-7 to GS-15 fireable, which will make them think twice before stalling conservative policies. Some of the most problematic bureaucrats in the federal government are the GS-13s, 14s, and 15s who wield significant power inside the administrative state. An executive order could enact this process within the various departments and agencies, but it would need to state clearly that it is OPM, not the various agencies, that gets to designate who is reclassified. Agencies can make recommendations, but the final call on who is reclassified is determined by the president's political appointees running OPM. While RIF exercises could effectively reduce the federal workforce by tens of thousands, maybe several hundred thousands, the Schedule F approach would be aimed at the more powerful government employees: a scalpel rather than a sledgehammer that could remove thousands of recalcitrant bureaucrats by reclassifying and then firing them.

All of the above are tools currently at the executive's disposal, but they should just be the start of the war on the administrative state. It must go beyond those steps. The FBI should cease to exist in its current form. Our Republic existed for nearly 120 years without it and would be far better today if the FBI was broken apart or at a bare minimum drastically reduced in size, perhaps only covering white-collar crime under a new name.

The Department of Justice must be reimagined and downsized. The NIH and the CDC must completely reformed, downsized, and actually turned into something useful for the future, albeit much smaller. The Consumer Financial Protection Bureau must be shut down and its building razed to the ground, its fields sowed with salt. For that matter, the Department of Energy should be shut down and its building personally imploded by the next Republican president, with a Freedom Park built over it. The exact same goes for HUD and Education. What better way to signal the end of the administrative state than to literally blow it up and sow its fields with salt?

It's time for an honest media, not the corporate propagandists and state stenographers masquerading as such. The entire point of a free and fair press is not an entity that amplifies whatever the administrative state or leftist regime wants, which is what we currently have. The point of a free, fair, and honest press, as intended by the Founders, is to shed light on whatever is taking place inside the halls of power so that the American people understand how the money and power they have delegated is being used. Then, in theory, those living in a representative democracy would be able to make informed decisions as to whether their elected leaders were faithful stewards of their delegated powers—and if not, they could replace them via the election process. But that fundamental aspect of a representative democracy—transparency, truth, and the free flow of information, enabling the American people to make informed decisions—is gone.

But that is the point, really. The administrative state doesn't want transparency because with transparency comes accountability. If there isn't a free a fair press shining the light on government, accountability can't exist; we certainly won't find it among our modern corporate propagandists and stenographers of the deep state. So one of the ways the propagandists can be reformed back into an honest media is to make them feel pain: through lawsuits and by removing the protections they've abused for decades, but also by fostering continued competition across all platforms, from TV to streaming, from news outlets to social media.

Where we are today is always where we were going to end up the minute Progressive Statism and the administrative state, with their rejection of natural rights, rejection of separation of powers, and hollowing out of the constitutional republic, were set in motion. From the flicking over of the first domino over a century ago, through a long series of one after another, the last one was always going to fall and end up here, right where we are presently in America. It was inevitable.

But what is *not* inevitable is what happens next: that is the next question we must ask, and it the question still to be answered. As it becomes increasingly hard to ignore reality, the American people, most of whom still have an innate decency and common sense when given enough facts, are going to have to decide: will they submit to the serfdom of the feudal administrative state, or will they realize yet again their legacy of being freeborn Americans living in a self-governing republic? "Ultimately, the defeat of administrative power will have to come from the people. Only their spirit of liberty can move Congress, inspire the president, and brace the judges to do their duty. Americans...need to recognize that administrative power revives absolute power and profoundly threatens civil liberties. Once Americans understand this, they can begin to push back, and the fate of administrative power will then only be a matter of time."[5]

All of what is taking place in America today is a tale as old as time: we're just the latest battlefield in the age-old struggle between whether Man or the state will gain dominance over the other, whether the modern version of Plato's Guardians and a Ruling Elite will rule a society or whether the people will govern themselves.

We must, however, be honest with ourselves. As President Ronald Reagan pointed out during his administration, in his study of history, "he was not aware of any nation that had turned away from bureaucratic statism after having gone as far as had the United States."[6] He said that nearly forty years ago, and the reinforcing coils of the American Leviathan have been building and strengthening ever since then, making the way back even harder. But then Reagan added, "Although no country has come back, I would like us to be the beginning; I would like us to be the first."[7] America was the first ever constitutional republic in the history of the world. Perhaps it can be the first to shake off the shackles of bureaucratic statism.

Yet this will only happen if the American people discover the truth and see the world as it truly is: that is the ultimate question that must be answered. Can we return to the original vision of the Founders? Can we restore the Republic? The answer is quite simple, albeit monumental in application: Break the State. Drain the Swamp. Restore the Republic.

ACKNOWLEDGEMENTS

No one ever truly writes a book by himself. Grant it, one must be inspired to actually write a draft of the book, but one can only take a manuscript so far without help from others. There are many who are involved: family and friends who give insights, feedback, and suggestions to take a manuscript to the next level. I have to thank my wife, Becca, for reading the draft of *American Leviathan* and giving me suggestions. I knew the book had a chance of being read by a greater audience once she'd read it and gotten fired up about the topic. I'd also like to thank my mother, Anne Ryun, who read and helped edit the book; my friends Ed McFadden and Mark Corallo, who gave me great suggestions on expanding the chapter on *Leviathan Today* to help highlight what a crushing beast Leviathan has become; and Kurt Schlichter, who went above and beyond what a busy friend needs to do, reading the manuscript in one weekend and making suggestions on how to expand the last chapter in regards to deconstructing the administrative state. Johnny McEntee and James Bacon deserve credit as well, for allowing me to use some of their ideas for the deconstruction of the administrative state in the final chapter of the book. And finally, Robert Erickson for doing the final editing of the book to ready it for publication.

WORKS CONSULTED

Bunker, Nick. *An Empire on the Edge: How Britain Came to Fight America.* New York: Vintage Books, 2014.

Carroll, Lewis. *Through the Looking Glass and What Alice Found There,* via The Project Gutenberg eBook: *https://www.gutenberg.org/files/12/12-h/12-h.htm.*

Cavendish, Richard. *Theodore Roosevelt Re-Elected President of the United States. History Today* 54, no. 11. *(November 2004).* https://www.history-today.com/richard-cavendish/theodore-roosevelt-re-elected-president-united-states.

Chevron U. S. A. Inc. v. Natural Resources Defense Council, Inc. Legal Information Institute, Cornell University. https://www.oyez.org/cases/1983/82-1005, accessed March 29, 2024.

Crichton, Michael. *State of Fear.* New York: HarperCollins, 2004.

Croly, Herbert. *The Promise of American Life.* New York: The Macmillan Company, 1911.

Debs, Eugene. "Speech of Acceptance," *International Socialist Review* (October, 1912). https://historymatters.gmu.edu/d/5725, accessed April 10, 2023.

Devine, Donald J. *Political Management of the Bureaucracy: A Guide to Reform and Control.* Ottawa, IL: Jameson Books, 2017.

Duros, Staci and Richard A. Champagne. *Discipline in the Wisconsin Legislature.* https://legis.wisconsin.gov/lrb/media/1182/discipline_in_wi_legis.pdf.

Eisenhower, Dwight D. "Farewell Address to the Nation." January 17, 1961. https://web.cs.ucdavis.edu/~rogaway/classes/188/materials eisenhower.pdf#:~:text=Three%20days%20from%20now%2C%20after%20a%20half%20century,a%20few%20final%20thoughts%20with%20you%2C%20my%20countrymen.

Hamburger, Philip A. *Chevron Bias,* 84 GEO. WASH. L. REV. 1187 (2016). Available at: https://scholarship.law.columbia.edu/faculty_scholarship/2768, p. 1203.

Hamburger, Philip. *The Administrative Threat*. New York: Encounter Books, 2018.

"Hepburn Rate Bill," The Center for Legislative Archives, US National Archives and Records Administration. *https://www.archives.gov/legislative/features/ hepburn.*

Hewitt, Hugh with Dr. West and Dr. Grant. "Hegel and Early Progressivism." *Hillsdale Dialogues* (blog). Hillsdale College, February 20, 2015. https:// blog.hillsdale.edu/dialogues/hegel-and-early-progressivism, accessed October 10, 2022.

La Follette, Robert. "The Danger Threatening Representative Government." Speeches of Robert M. La Follette, Wisconsin Historical Society, accessed June 16, 2024, https://www.wisconsinhistory.org/pdfs/lessons/EDU-SpeechTranscript-SpeechesLaFollette-DangerThreatening.pdf.

Leonard, Thomas. *Illiberal Reformers: Race, Eugenics & American Economics in the Progressive Era*. Princeton: Princeton University Press, 2016.

Lindsley, Art. "C.S. Lewis on Chronological Snobbery." (Arlington, VA: The C. S. Lewis Institute). https://www.cslewisinstitute.org/wp-content/uploads/KD-2003-Spring-C.S.-Lewis-on-Chronological-Snobbery-596.pdf.

Lyman, Brianna. "Hillary Clinton And Russia Hoax Architect Warn Of GOP 'Disinformation Campaigns,' *The Federalist*, April 23, 2024, https://thefederalist.com/2024/04/23/hillary-clinton-and-russia-hoax-architect-warn-of-gop-disinformation-campaigns/.

Mitchell, Ellen. "Defense Department Fails Another Audit, but Makes Progress," *The Hill*, November 17, 2022.

Pearson, Sidney. *Herbert D. Croly: Apostle of Progressivism* Washington, DC: The Heritage Foundation, March 14, 2013. https://www.heritage.org/political-process/report/herbert-d-croly-apostle-progressivism.

Marini, John, ed. Ken Masugi. *Unmasking the Administrative State: The Crisis of American Politics in the Twenty-First Century*. New York: Encounter Books, 2019.

Milkis, Sidney. *Theodore Roosevelt, the Progressive Party, and the Transformation of American Democracy*. Lawrence, KS: University Press of Kansas, 2009.

Nelson, Steven. "FBI Chief Christopher Wray Admits Ditching Hearing for Vacay on Bureau Jet," *New York Post*, November 17, 2022. https://nypost.com/2022/11/17/fbi-chief-wray-admits-ditching-hearing-for-vacay-on-bureau-jet/.

Pestritto, Ronald J. and William J. Atto, eds. *American Progressivism; A Reader*. Lanham, MD: Lexington Books, 2008.

Pestritto, Ronald J. *America Transformed: The Rise and Legacy of American Progressivism*. New York: Encounter Books, 2021.

Popper, Karl. *The Open Society and Its Enemies*, 5th ed. New York: Routledge, 1966.

Roosevelt, Theodore. *Social Justice and Popular Rule; Essays, Addresses and Public Statements Relating to the Progressive Movement (1910-1916)*. New York: Charles Scribner's Sons, 1925.

Reardon, Tony. "Federal Employees Want You to Keep Your Politics Out of Their Work," *The Hill*, August 4, 2023.

Ryun, Ned. *Restoring Our Republic: The Making of the Republic and How We Reclaim It*. Amazon Publishing, 2019.

Schaeffer, Francis. *How Should We Then Live? The Rise and Decline of Western Thought and Culture*. Wheaton, IL: Crossway Books, 1976.

Smith, Ralph. "Average $90,510 Federal Employee Salary and Other Traits of 2.1 Million+ Federal Employees," Fedsmith.com, May 10, 2021.

Sowell, Thomas. "There Are No Solutions, Only Trade-offs." https://www.youtube.com/watch?v=3_EtIWmja-4.

Swan, Jonathan. "Government Workers Shun Trump, Give Big Money to Clinton," *The Hill*, October 26, 2016. https://thehill.com/homenews/campaign/302817-government-workers-shun-trump-give-big-money-to-clinton-campaign/.

Taft, William Howard. "On Popular Unrest," History Matters. https://history-matters.gmu.edu/d/5724/, accessed April 10, 2023.

Tate, Kristin. "The Sheer Size of Our Government Workforce Is an Alarming Problem," *The Hill*, April 14, 2019.

Truman, Harry S. "Limit CIA Role To Intelligence," *The Washington Post*, December 22, 1963. https://www.cia.gov/readingroom/docs/CIA-RDP75-00149R000700550045-9.pdf.

Wall Street Journal Editorial Board. "The IRS Is About to Go Beast Mode," *The Wall Street Journal*, August 2, 2022. https://www.wsj.com/articles/the-irs-is-about-to-go-beast-mode-chuck-schumer-joe-manchin-audit-taxes-middle-class-joe-biden-11659477320?mod=itp_wsj&ru=yahoo.

Whitman, James Q. *Hitler's American Model: The United States and the Making of Nazi Race Law*. Princeton: Princeton University Press, 2017.

Wilson, Woodrow. "The Author and Signers of the Declaration of Independence," in Pestritto, *Wilson: Essential Political Writings*, pp. 97–105.

Wire, Sarah D. "the Government Spends $1.7 Billion a Year on 770,000 Empty Buildings, and One Central Valley Congressman Is Fed Up," *Los Angeles Times*, March 3, 2016. https://www.latimes.com/politics/la-pol-ca-jeff-denham-government-property-bill-20160303-story.html.

Yarbrough, Jean M. *Theodore Roosevelt: Progressive Crusader* Washington, DC: The Heritage Foundation, September 24, 2012. https://www.heritage.org/political-process/report/theodore-roosevelt-progressive-crusader.

Zamost, Scott and Contessa Brewer. "Inside the Mind of Criminals: How to Brazenly Steal $100 Billion from Medicare and Medicaid," CNBC, March 9, 2023. https://www.cnbc.com/2023/03/09/how-medicare-and-medicaid-fraud-became-a-100b-problem-for-the-us.html.

NOTES

CHAPTER ONE

1 Brianna Lyman, "Hillary Clinton And Russia Hoax Architect Warn Of GOP 'Disinformation Campaigns,'" *The Federalist*, April 23, 2024, https://thefederalist.com/2024/04/23/hillary-clinton-and-russia-hoax-architect-warn-of-gop-disinformation-campaigns/.

CHAPTER TWO

1 Pestritto, Ronald J. And William J. Atto, eds., *American Progressivism; A Reader* (Lanham, MD: Lexington Books, 2008), 195.

2 Ibid., 197.

3 Ibid., 206.

CHAPTER THREE

1 Robert La Follette, "The Danger Threatening Representative Government," Speeches of Robert M. La Follette, Wisconsin Historical Society, accessed June 16, 2024, https://www.wisconsinhistory.org/pdfs/lessons/EDU-SpeechTranscript-SpeechesLaFollette-DangerThreatening.pdf.

2 Ibid.

3 Ibid.

4 Ibid.

5 Staci Duros and Richard A. Champagne, *Discipline in the Wisconsin Legislature, Wisconsin History Project* 2, no 2, (June 2020), https://legis.wisconsin.gov/lrb/media/1182/discipline_in_wi_legis.pdf.

6 Thomas Leonard, *Illiberal Reformers: Race, Eugenics & American Economics in the Progressive Era* (Princeton, NJ: Princeton University Press, 2016), 52.

7 Ibid., 41.

8 Ibid., 42.

9 "17th Amendment to the US Constitution: Direct Election of Senators," (Washington, DC: National Archives), https://www.archives.gov/milestone-documents/17th-amendment#:~:text=In%201910%20and%201911%2C%20the,of%20racial%20discrimination%20among%20voters.

CHAPTER FOUR

1 Ronald J. Pestritto, *America Transformed: The Rise and Legacy of American Progressivism* (New York: Encounter Books, 2021), 134.

2 Herbert Croly, *The Promise of American Life* (New York: The Macmillan Company, 1911), via The Project Gutenberg eBook, https://www.gutenberg.org/files/14422/14422-h/14422-h.htm#CHAPTER_I.

3 Sidney Pearson, *Herbert D. Croly: Apostle of Progressivism,* (Washington, DC: The Heritage Foundation, March 14, 2013), https://www.heritage.org/political-process/report/herbert-d-croly-apostle-progressivism.

4 Pestritto and Atto, 21.

5 Pestritto, 41.

6 John Marini, ed. by Ken Masugi, *Unmasking the Administrative State: The Crisis of American Politics in the Twenty-First Century* (New York: Encounter Books, 2019), 52.

7 Pearson, Herbert D. "Croly: Apostle of Progressivism (Washington, DC: The Heritage Foundation, March 14, 2013), https://www.heritage.org/political-process/report/herbert-d-croly-apostle-progressivism.

CHAPTER FIVE

1 Richard Cavendish, "Theodore Roosevelt Re-Elected President of the United States," *History Today,* 54, no. 11, (November 2004), https://www.historytoday.com/richard-cavendish/theodore-roosevelt-re-elected-president-united-states.

2 The Center for Legislative Archives, US National Archives, "Hepburn Rate Bill," https://www.archives.gov/legislative/features/hepburn

3 Jean M. Yarbrough, *Theodore Roosevelt: Progressive Crusader,* (Washington, DC: The Heritage Foundation, September 24, 2012), *https://www.heritage.org/political-process/report/theodore-roosevelt-progressive-crusader.*

4 Sidney M. Milkis, *Theodore Roosevelt, the Progressive Party and the Transformation of American Democracy* (Lawrence, KS: University of Press of Kansas, 2009), 160.

5 Pestritto and Atto, 217.

6 Yarbrough, *Theodore Roosevelt.*

7 Ibid.

8 Ibid.

9 Ibid.

10 Milkis, 54.

CHAPTER SIX

1 Milkis., 55.

2 Ibid., 61.

3 Theodore Roosevelt, *Social Justice and Popular Rule; Essays, Addresses and Public Statements Relating to the Progressive Movement (1910-1916)* (New York: Charles Scribner's Sons, 1925), 363, 368.

4 Ibid., 411.

5 Milkis, 152.

6 Ibid., 233.

7 Ibid., 230.

8 William Howard Taft, "On Popular Unrest," History Matters, https://historymatters.gmu.edu/d/5724/, accessed April 10, 2023.

9 Milkis, 226.

10 Ibid., 219.

11 Eugene Debs, "Speech of Acceptance," *International Socialist Review* (October 1912), https://historymatters.gmu.edu/d/5725, accessed April 10, 2023.

12 Leonard, x.

13 Ibid., 54.

CHAPTER SEVEN

1 Pestritto and Atto, 6.

2 Leonard, 65.

3 David Hanson, "KKK and WCTU: Partners in Prohibition," Leben, July 20, 2012, https://leben.us/kkk-wctu-partners-prohibition/.

CHAPTER EIGHT

1 Woodrow Wilson, "The Author and Signers of the Declaration of Independence," in Pestritto, *Wilson: Essential Political Writings*, 97–105.

2 Art Lindsley, "C.S. Lewis on Chronological Snobbery," (Springfield, VA: The C. S. Lewis Institute, April 16, 2013), https://www.cslewisinstitute.org/wp-content/uploads/KD-2003-Spring-C.S.-Lewis-on-Chronological-Snobbery-596.pdf.

3 Pestritto, 81.

4 Pestritto and Atto, 50–51.

5 Ned Ryun, *Restoring Our Republic: The Making of the Republic and How We Reclaim It* (Amazon Publishing, 2019), 167.

6 Pestritto and Atto, 55.

7 Ibid., 4.

8 I*bid.*, 56.

9 Ibid., 62.

10 Marini, 101.

11 Pestritto, 27.

12 Pestritto and Atto, 107.

13 Ibid., 119.

14 Ibid., 122.

15 Ibid.

16 Croly, 18.

17 Ibid., 23.

18 Leonard, 191.

CHAPTER NINE

1 Karl Popper, *The Open Society and Its Enemies* (New York: Routledge, 1966), 237.

2 Hugh Hewitt, Dr. Thomas West and Dr. John Grant, "Hegel and Early Progressivism," *Hillsdale Dialogues* (blog), Hillsdale College, February 20, 2015, accessed October 10, 2022.

3 Popper, 246.

4 Ibid., 250.

5 Ibid., 256.

6 Marini, 228.

7 Hewitt, West, and Grant.

8 Marini, 100.

9 Pestritto, 26.

10 Leonard, 13.

11 Popper, 262.

CHAPTER TEN

1 Pestritto, 22.

2 Pestritto, 24.

3 Ryun, 187.

4 Dwayne Walls Jr., "Reflecting on the Revolution," *Chatham News & Record,* July 7, 2021, https://chathamnewsrecord.com/stories/reflecting-on-the-revolution,9787.

5 Francis Schaeffer, *How Should We Then Live? The Rise and Decline of Western Thought and Culture* (Wheaton, IL: Crossway Books, 1976), 239.

6 Don Devine, *Political Management of the Bureaucracy; A Guide to Reform and Control* (Ottawa, IL: Jameson Books, 2017), 90.

7 Leonard, 16.

8 Ibid.

9 Nick Bunker, *An Empire on the Edge: How Britain Came to Fight America* (New York: Vintage Books, 2014), 311, 313.

10 Leonard, 106.

11 Marini, 79.

12 Schaeffer, 242.

13 Pestritto and Atto, 137.

CHAPTER ELEVEN

1 "Lyndon B. Johnson, Remarks at the University of Michigan, May 22, 1964," The American Presidency Project, University of California Santa Barbara, https://www.presidency.ucsb.edu/documents/remarks-the-university-michigan.

2 Marini, 41.

3 Ibid., 23-24.

4 *Chevron U. S. A. Inc. v. Natural Resources Defense Council, Inc.* from the website of the Legal Information Institute, Cornell Law School, https://www.oyez.org/cases/1983/82-1005, accessed March 29, 2024.

5 Ibid.

6 Philip A. Hamburger, Chevron Bias, 84 GEO. WASH. L. REV. 1187 (2016). Available at: https://scholarship.law.columbia.edu/faculty_scholarship/2768, 1203.

7 Ibid.

8 Ibid.

9 Ibid.

10 Philip Hamburger, *The Administrative Threat* (New York: Encounter Books, 2018), 23–24.

11 Marini, 147.

CHAPTER TWELVE

1 Richard M. Ketchum, *Saratoga: Turning Point of America's Revolutionary War* (New York: Henry Holt and Co., 1997) 65.

2 Lewis Carroll, *Through the Looking Glass and What Alice Found There,* via The Project Gutenberg eBook: *https://www.gutenberg.org/files/12/12-h/12-h.htm.*

3 "Joseph Goebbels: On the 'Big Lie,'" Jewish Virtual Library, accessed June 16, 2024, https://www.jewishvirtuallibrary.org/joseph-goebbels-on-the-quot-big-lie-quot.

4 Schaeffer, 26.

5 Schaeffer, 145.

6 Ibid., 224.

7 Ibid., 145.

8 L. Frank Baum, *The Wonderful Wizard of Oz*, via Project Gutenberg, https://www.gutenberg.org/files/55/55-h/55-h.htm#chap15.

9 Leonard, 101–02.

10 Michael Crichton, *State of Fear* (New York: HarperCollins, 2004), 575–76.

11 Leonard, 121.

12 Ibid.

13 Marini, 245.

14 Ibid., 108.

15 Ibid., 149.

16 Ibid., 165.

17 Crichton, 577.

18 Ibid.

CHAPTER THIRTEEN

1 Pestritto, 190.

2 Devine, 90.

3 Marini, 57.

4 Pestritto, 201.

5 Marini, 129.

6 Ibid., 143.

7 Ibid., 145.

8 Ibid., 48.

CHAPTER FOURTEEN

1 Popper, 261.

2 "Dwight D. Eisenhower's Farewell Address to the Nation, January 17, 1961," available at the University of California, Davis, website, https://web.cs.ucdavis.edu/~rogaway/classes/188/materials/eisenhower.pdf#:~:text=Three%20days%20from%20now%2C%20after%20a%20half%20century,a%20few%20final%20thoughts%20with%20you%2C%20my%20countrymen.

CHAPTER FIFTEEN

1 Clyde Wayne Crews Jr., "How Many Federal Agencies Exist? We Can't Drain The Swamp Until We Know," *Forbes*, June 5, 2017, https://www.forbes.com/sites/waynecrews/2017/07/05/how-many-federal-agencies-exist-we-cant-drain-the-swamp-until-we-know/.

2 Kristin Tate, "The Sheer Size of our Government Workforce Is an Alarming Problem," *The Hill*, April 14, 2019.

3 Ralph Smith, "Average $90,510 Federal Employee Salary and Other Traits of 2.1 Million+ Federal Employees," Fedsmith.com, May 10, 2021.

4 Ellen Mitchell, "Defense Department Fails Another Audit, but Makes Progress," *The Hill*, November 17, 2022.

5 Hope Yen, "Buttigieg Launches $1B Pilot to Build Racial Equity in Roads," *The Associated Press*, June 30, 2022. https://apnews.com/article/race-and-ethnicity-racial-injustice-transportation-pete-buttigieg-48e09f253781c89359d875f19fc70f9d.

6 Sarah D. Wire, "The Government Spends $1.7 Billion a Year on 770,000 Empty Buildings, and One Central Valley Congressman Is Fed Up," *Los Angeles Times*, March 3, 2016. https://www.latimes.com/politics/la-pol-ca-jeff-denham-government-property-bill-20160303-story.html.

7 Scott Zamost and Contessa Brewer, "Inside the Mind of Criminals: How to Brazenly Steal $100 Billion from Medicare and Medicaid," CNBC, March 9, 2023. https://www.cnbc.com/2023/03/09/how-medicare-and-medicaid-fraud-became-a-100b-problem-for-the-us.html.

8 Wall Street Journal Editorial Board, "The IRS Is About to Go Beast Mode," *The Wall Street Journal*, August 2, 2022. https://www.wsj.com/articles/the-

irs-is-about-to-go-beast-mode-chuck-schumer-joe-manchin-audit-taxes-middle-class-joe-biden-11659477320?mod=itp_wsj&ru=yahoo.

9 Steven Nelson, "FBI Chief Christopher Wray Admits Ditching Hearing for Vacay on Bureau Jet," *New York Post*, November 17, 2022. https://nypost.com/2022/11/17/fbi-chief-wray-admits-ditching-hearing-for-vacay-on-bureau-jet/.

10 Madeline Osburn, "4 Different Lies James Clapper Told About Lying To Congress," *The Federalist*, March 6, 2019. https://thefederalist.com/2019/03/06/four-different-lies-james-clapper-told-about-lying-to-congress/.

11 Harry S. Truman, "Limit CIA Role To Intelligence," *The Washington Post*, Dec. 22, 1963, https://www.cia.gov/readingroom/docs/CIA-RDP75-00149R000700550045-9.pdf.

CHAPTER SIXTEEN

1 Thomas Sowell, "There Are No Solutions, Only Trade-offs," *Fox News*, August, 10, 2013, https://www.youtube.com/watch?v=3_EtIWmja-4.

2 Tony Reardon, "Federal Employees Want You to Keep Your Politics out of Their Work," *The Hill*, August 4, 2023, https://thehill.com/opinion/finance/4131121-federal-employees-want-you-to-keep-your-politics-out-of-their-work/.

3 Hamburger, 62.

4 Jonathan Swan, "Government Workers Shun Trump, Give Big Money to Clinton," *The Hill*, October 26, 2016. https://thehill.com/homenews/campaign/302817-government-workers-shun-trump-give-big-money-to-clinton-campaign/.

5 Ibid., 64.

6 Devine, 155.

7 Ibid., 155-156.